T0300321

ROUTLEDGE LIBRARY EDITIONS:
WORK & SOCIETY

Volume 7

EMPLOYMENT
AND
THE DEPRESSED AREAS

EMPLOYMENT
AND
THE DEPRESSED AREAS

H. POWYS GREENWOOD

Routledge
Taylor & Francis Group

LONDON AND NEW YORK

First published in 1936 by George Routledge & Sons Ltd.

This edition first published in 2024
by Routledge
4 Park Square, Milton Park, Abingdon, Oxon OX14 4RN

and by Routledge
605 Third Avenue, New York, NY 10158

Routledge is an imprint of the Taylor & Francis Group, an informa business

© 1936 H. Powys Greenwood/George Routledge & Sons Ltd.

British Library Cataloguing in Publication Data
A catalogue record for this book is available from the British Library

ISBN: 978-1-032-80236-7 (Set)
ISBN: 978-1-032-81351-6 (Volume 7) (hbk)
ISBN: 978-1-032-81353-0 (Volume 7) (pbk)
ISBN: 978-1-003-49933-6 (Volume 7) (ebk)

DOI: 10.4324/9781003499336

Publisher's Note
The publisher has gone to great lengths to ensure the quality of this reprint but points out that some imperfections in the original copies may be apparent.

Disclaimer
The publisher has made every effort to trace copyright holders and would welcome correspondence from those they have been unable to trace.

EMPLOYMENT
AND
THE DEPRESSED AREAS

by

H. POWYS GREENWOOD

LONDON
GEORGE ROUTLEDGE & SONS, LTD.
BROADWAY HOUSE, 68–74 CARTER LANE, E.C.
1936

TO MY FRIENDS IN WEST CUMBERLAND
WHO OPENED MY EYES

CONTENTS

vii

Contents

Not a comprehensive plan—aim to suggest a method—
only " enterprises for purposes of gain " of real use—how
can they be stimulated—a definite incentive essential—
the Special Areas Reconstruction Association and its
limitations—essential to " back the man "—and to find
him—the Development Councils—how they could be
more effective—a Finance Company—how to mobilize
goodwill—immigrant industrialists—effective publicity
—need to make areas attractive to business men—
trading estates—transport and public facilities—social
atmosphere—residential and holiday centres—West
Cumberland suitable for experiment—comprehensive
action needed—rearmament and strategic considerations
—everybody can help—social leaders and the great
families—the function of social service—need for co-
operation with productive enterprise and administration
—labour transference—obstructionism fatal—spirit of a
crusade needed.

Suggestions not exhaustive—meant to point the way—
three fundamental points—problem of employment vital
—should be tackled in depressed areas—by stimulating
productive enterprise—great effect on employment as a
whole likely—Beveridge's gloomy prophecy—Keynes
again—depressed areas a microcosm of the nation—
successful experiment would point the way to solution of
problems of enterprise—and of government—social
control of economic life—a " lead " to the world.

PREFACE

Iᴛ is perhaps unnecessary to make any excuse for adding another book on the problem of employment to the many already in existence. For although the subject has been exhaustively discussed from almost every conceivable point of view we cannot claim, with over one and a half million registered unemployed and a good many more unregistered sufferers, to have gone far towards solving it.

As the title indicates, I have endeavoured to attack the problem from the positive angle, as one of employment rather than of unemployment. How can employment be stimulated; indeed how can the immense frustrated energies now running to seed in our civilization, and not only among the technically " unemployed," be directed into useful channels ?

I do not pretend to have found the final answer to this much-disputed and complicated question, whether in the form of a theoretical system or otherwise. What I am suggesting is primarily a method, the same method of experimental trial and error upon which that greatest of all recent human achievements, modern science, is based.

There can be no doubt about the most suitable places for experiment in providing employment. The depressed areas remain little islands of worklessness

and consequent misery barely touched by the rising
tide of prosperity. In certain districts, which have
been scheduled as " Special Areas " and include by no
means all the depressed parts of the country, the
National Government has admitted a case for special
action.

But its efforts have hitherto been very largely
ineffective. In the chapter headed " The Depressed
Areas—Tragedy," I have tried to explain why this was
so, and the subsequent chapters contain some practical
suggestions for immediate action and indicate the
fundamental principles upon which I believe this action
should be based. Finally, I have given reasons for the
hope that a successful experiment in stimulating
economic activity and employment in the depressed
areas will point the way to the mastery of these
problems over a far wider field.

Throughout the book I have made extensive, though
I hope not unscrupulous, use of works on unemployment and kindred subjects, as well as of official reports,
and have quoted many passages verbatim. I trust
those concerned will accept the acknowledgments contained in the text and will forgive me for not having
asked their permission in individual cases. Thanks are
also due to Sir Edward Penton, K.B.E., and to Mr. J. A.
Dale, C.B.E., of the Ministry of Labour, for their kind-
ness in going over the proofs, and above all to my
friends in West Cumberland, to whom my work is
dedicated.

Had it not been for those friends, had it not been for
my brief period of social service in that lovely part of
England, this book would never have been written.
Drawn originally to the study of unemployment by

some personal experience of the bitter sense of not being able to fit in anywhere, it was not until I went to Cumberland that I realized what I wanted to say.

Now that I have said it I am fully aware of the gaps in the argument and the shortcomings of its presentation. To some extent they were unavoidable in a brief study of this kind. But if the book has some effect towards inducing effective action on behalf of men as staunch under adversity as any I have ever met, it will not have been written in vain.

EMPLOYMENT AND THE
DEPRESSED AREAS

CHAPTER I

HISTORICAL PERSPECTIVES

THE problem of employment is as old as human life itself. It is the problem of subsistence—" in the sweat of thy face shalt thou eat bread "—and it is the problem of " self-expression," to use a more modern phrase, of how to bring human talents to their fullest and most satisfying use. It is the problem which most exercises the minds of parents and children ; is not the most common question put to a child : " What are you going to be when you grow up ? " It is the problem which lies at the root of most wars, for even when they are not the result of a struggle for subsistence, for economic opportunity, they are generally due to surplus energy in some form, to men seeking new scope for their activities, new fields to conquer. And it is the problem which the progressive modern world, with its industrial and scientific civilization, has been least successful in solving.

Unemployment is merely the negative aspect, the reverse side of the medal. It is in a sense a newer problem. But while it is safe to say that it has never been of such absorbing importance as to-day—the older economists give it little or no space—its origins can none the less be traced back to the earliest times.

Unemployment is chiefly a problem arising out of the

division of labour. As Sir Norman Angell and Mr. Harold Wright have pointed out in their book *Can Governments Cure Unemployment?* as soon as there is division of labour, as soon, for example, as a village develops and one of the peasants becomes a blacksmith, no longer growing his own food but depending on getting it in exchange for the billhooks or hoes which he makes, then he is likely to face unemployment when the peasants have all the hoes they need. Unless he can obtain land to till or find someone to employ him to do so, he may well starve in the midst of plenty. There must be well over twenty million such blacksmiths in the world to-day, trade recovery notwithstanding.

But this is not quite the whole story. Angell and Wright, it is true, contrast the state of the blacksmith with that of the primitive self-supporting peasant family, which they maintain to be free from unemployment. Yet, after all, if a self-supporting family is living on a piece of land of limited fertility and its numbers grow to more than the land can support, the head of the family, finding that the work put in by the best efficient members does not produce sufficient for their subsistence, may very well turn them out into the desert to fend for themselves. In this pressure of population on the means of subsistence lies the origin of the poverty and beggary (unemployment in another form) in such countries as India and China.

Nearly all authorities agree, however, that this question of shortage of living room has been displaced by the achievements of modern science and technique from its earlier position of importance. But it has another theoretical aspect which has been stressed by many economists, notably Sir William Beveridge and Professor Robbins. Professor Robbins gives as an illustration a peasant family supporting itself by tilling three fields of unequal fertility, each of which, however, demands the same time and effort for its cultivation. At a given moment the family decide that the return for their effort on the least fertile field (their wages) is insufficient and that they will no longer cultivate it. Then either a third of their number will be unemployed, or they will all be unemployed for a third of their available time. Sir William Beveridge regards this illustration as conclusive evidence that insistence on a certain standard of living may on occasion be a cause of unemployment under any economic system.

The history of employment fluctuations, so far as it is known, bears out this rough analysis. Under slave-owning systems, such as those of Greece and Rome, there seems to have been practically no unemployment. A slave cannot assert a claim to any standard of living, and when he is no longer needed in his job owing to a breakdown in the division of labour or to lack of available subsistence, he is sold and turned on to any work that comes along. It was not until a class of proletarian freemen had developed in Rome, partly owing to the displacement of the free peasantry by cheap slave labour, that we hear of " bread and circuses," the Roman equivalent of " the dole." Like modern governments, the Roman emperors took the line of least resistance. They kept the unemployed from starving and attempted to provide diversions to take their minds off their troubles instead of finding them work.

The condition of the masses of the people after the downfall of the Roman Empire and the break-up of its economic system must remain largely a matter for historical speculation. Mr. George Whitehead, in his book *Unemployment—Its Causes and Remedies*, suggests that millions of slaves were scattered with neither masters nor means of support. They may thus well have welcomed the opportunity of becoming slaves, or rather serfs, of the Catholic Church, and working on the lands of the abbeys and monasteries which began to be erected with the aid of serf labour, or of being impressed into the service of the developing feudal nobility.

Gradually the economic system of the Middle Ages was evolved, and for close on five centuries it provided a certain measure of security. Whatever acts of oppression the barons may have been guilty of, they did assure a livelihood of sorts to their serfs ; indeed, Mr. Stirling Taylor, in his remarkable *Modern History of England*, suggests that their function as the armed servants of the nation, the local guards of their tenants, and the administrative and judicial authorities of their lands, put them on a higher plane of usefulness than many modern owners. " It is more arduous," he writes, " to defend and govern one's tenants than to collect rents ; which obvious fact has been recognized by most historians."

In the towns, too, the guild system gave some security to the workers or craftsmen, to the men who created some of the finest architectural monuments of any age—the mediæval cathedrals ; while those who were unable to find land or service under a baron or entry into a guild could turn to the charity of the churches or monasteries. Thus, in spite of wars,

pestilences and famines, in spite of great pressure on
the means of subsistence, there seems to have been
little uncared-for unemployment, and there is no need
to fall into the error of over-idealizing the " Age of
Faith " to admit that the life led by the masses of the
people was not only incomparably better than in the
disturbed period after the fall of Rome, but had certain
inherently praiseworthy features of its own.

The first signs of large-scale unemployment of a more
or less modern type became visible when the feudal
economic system began to break up under the Tudors.
And here we come to an aspect of unemployment which
is of great importance to-day—the great dislocation in
the normal division of labour which inevitably accom-
panies transition from one economic system to another.

With Bosworth field and the accession of Henry VII
in 1485, the Middle Ages in England may be said to
have been at an end. The centralized Tudor Government replaced the local government of the barons, and
the great development of the wool trade began the
conversion of feudal landlords into capitalists. With
the Wars of the Roses the old nobility had virtually
destroyed itself, but new men were coming up whose
aim was economic power and wealth—men who did not
hesitate ruthlessly to turn out peasants in order to make
room for the more profitable sheep-runs. The same
men began that enclosure of common lands which,
whatever its economic justification, will always remain
a blot on English social history. At the same time the
monasteries were despoiled—largely for the benefit of
these new men—and the impoverished were left without
their customary means of support. Hundreds of
thousands of destitute and masterless men overran the

country—Henry VIII is said to have had seventy-two thousand " idle persons and great and small thieves " consigned to the gallows.

Gradually the displaced peasants settled down in the new trades which developed during that exuberant age, but throughout the sixteenth century economic fluctuations were acute enough to produce a great deal of unemployment from time to time. The Government attempted by a system of admonition, not unlike that of Nazi Germany, to induce property-owners to make adequate charitable provision for the workless. But this proved wholly insufficient, and in 1601 each parish was compelled by law to provide work for the able-bodied and subsistence for the non-able-bodied by levying a rate on property. This was the famous Elizabethan Poor Law, which held the field for over two centuries.

The next period of catastrophic unemployment was due to another transition—that of the Industrial Revolution. The development of the modern industrial system and the appalling distress by which it was first accompanied have been recorded in hundreds of histories and text-books. Towards the end of the eighteenth century pauperism and unemployment reached unprecedented levels. In those days war did not involve a tremendous demand for man-power, and the Napoleonic wars, unlike the last war, greatly accentuated the trouble. The fear of revolution led to a great extension of relief, the cost of which was doubled by an Act permitting out-relief in 1796. At about the same time the Berkshire magistrates, appalled by the distress among the rural population which resulted from the decay of cottage industries, granted an allowance out of the Poor Rate to cover the loss of money formerly made by home spinning. This was the famous Speenhamland Act which led to the wholesale subsidizing of wages. The inevitable result was to encourage employers to keep wages below a subsistence level in the assurance that the parish would always make up the deficiency.

The Speenhamland Act is generally attacked as a piece of economic insanity, and it undoubtedly produced a great many ill effects—the cost of relief rising to what was then regarded as the astronomical figure of eight million pounds. None the less it was a humane measure which mitigated to some extent the appalling conditions of the peasantry and working classes. Whitehead suggests that its worst feature was the failure invariably to insist on the compulsory work test, but most other authorities maintain that the notorious abuses of the Poor Law at that period were due even more to the besetting desire if possible to require some task of work from the recipients of relief. Unemployed men were actually harnessed to parish carts, and one Poor Law overseer in Kent made an unemployed shepherd walk twenty-six miles every day for his money.

There is no doubt that by 1830 some measure to put the administration on a more economic basis had become essential. Nevertheless the principles laid down by the Poor Law Commissioners in 1832–34 were so lacking in humanity that they have rarely been completely enforced. The first principle was that relief should not be offered to the able-bodied and their families except in the workhouse, and the second that the lot of the able-bodied should be made " less eligible " than that of the lowest class of independent wage-earner.   Disraeli's opinion on this matter is worth quoting :   " to suppose for a moment that in a highly-civilized country the poor population should be controlled and managed by shutting them up in prison, was to support that which was contrary to every principle of humane society.   No other term than that of imprisonment could be given to the confinement which the poor underwent in the Union workhouses."

The principle of " less eligibility " was frankly penal. The fact that it was necessary to have recourse to it in order to drive the workers into the new factories is the best measure of the conditions prevailing there.   It was obviously no easy matter to make existence in the workhouses " less eligible " than in the industrial towns, where vast multitudes of men, women and children were made to toil and strain for twelve, fourteen and even sixteen hours a day, often for less than a bare subsistence, and under such wretched and insanitary conditions that they will remain a by-word for all time.

The Poor Law was the first-fruit of the Reform Bill, which admitted the rising class of manufacturers to power.   Together they mark the complete victory of modern capitalism.

This book is not intended as an addition to the mass of literature defending or attacking the system of capitalist ownership under which we are still living ; my purpose in writing it is to analyse some of the problems of employment and to put forward practical remedies which can be adopted by men of goodwill within the existing system, whatever views they may hold about the ideal form of society. But here I must make two points of a general nature about which there will be little dispute.

Nineteenth-century capitalism played a part in the history of man's conquest over Nature which probably no other system could have played. It was the mainspring of a technical progress unparalleled in history ; it opened up the raw materials and markets of the whole world to energy and enterprise ; it vastly increased the national wealth of Britain as well as of other nations —although at the same time increasing the inequity of its distribution ; it led to an increase in productive capacity which seemed to make a reasonable subsistence for all possible for the first time in history ; and it enabled a vast increase of population coupled with a great rise in the standard of living not merely of the capitalists but of the people as a whole.

But the new system, with its dogma of free enterprise and its substitution for the independent craftsman (who at any rate had owned his tools) of the factory worker with no control of the means of production and little of his own life, placed the security of the vast majority of the people at the mercy of impersonal economic forces which neither they nor their rulers could fully understand or control. The early capitalists were revolutionaries who, in alliance with Adam Smith and his successors, ruthlessly destroyed in the name of *laissez-faire* practically all the mechanism for the regulation and planning of trade and production with which governments, guilds, corporations and individuals had endeavoured to maintain security of livelihood. " It is worth notice," writes Sidney Webb in *The Decay of Capitalist Civilization*, " that the insurgent capitalist *entrepreneurs* in the century of their exuberance were in another respect analogous to Bakunin the anarchist and Lenin the communist, who in the Russia of 1918–19 had the opportunity of putting into practice so much of the spirit of Bakunin's teaching. They were absolutely ruthless in the clearance that was made of everything that stood in the way of the carrying out of their ideas of social reorganization—neither weighing in the balance the incidental advantages of the system that they considered obsolete, nor heeding the suffering that their revolution caused to individuals without number—and, what should never be forgotten, making no compensation whatever for the breach of legally ' established expectations ' of the uncounted multitude of innocent persons whose incomes were annihilated and whose very livelihood was destroyed by the revolution that they had brought about." In more recent times, nations which have gone the same way seem to have had a similar experience, and Webb records a casual observation by an astute Japanese statesman that " the introduction of the capitalist system into Japan had brought in its train an ever-growing class of destitute persons—a class quite unknown in the old Japan of the daimio and rice cultivator."

It may be suggested that such dislocation and destitution is an inevitable feature of all revolutions. However that may be, even during the prosperous nineteenth century, with its expanding wealth and rising demand for labour, insecurity remained the lot of a large proportion of the population. At intervals throughout the nineteenth century the depressions of the " trade cycle " threw hundreds of thousands, if not millions, of men out of work through no fault of their own, and though unemployment does not seem to have been as obstinate or as vast a problem as it is to-day, that is at any rate to a considerable extent due to the lack of statistical means of measuring it and to the fact that the working masses were less vocal than they have become since the rise of Trade Unions and the development of education.

Almost immediately after the new Poor Law was passed, special permission had to be given to London and other towns to resume the payment of out-relief to the destitute unemployed. Even nineteenth-century governments could not sum up the hardness of heart fully to apply the principle of " less eligibility " to the victims of the recurring industrial depressions. For the next eighty years the nation, haunted by an uneasy conscience, continued to apply piecemeal remedies while remaining unwilling to relax the Poor Law principles as a whole. These piecemeal remedies fall into three categories—charity, relief works and Trade Union insurance.

At most of the recurring crises of unemployment relief funds were opened. " The money was spent," writes Mr. R. C. Davison, in his work *The Unemployed*, " and may in the balance have done more good than harm, but that is the best to be said of it." Sometimes it was merely scrambled for indiscriminately, sometimes it was doled out in a more orderly manner. The Charity Organization Society, founded in 1869, did succeed in bringing some order into chaos. It was a permanent organization, and its local secretaries gradually gained sufficient experience of the working classes and their problems to prevent the worst forms of waste and demoralization. Relief was generally given in kind rather than in money ; for example, a craftsman might be re-equipped with tools or restored to his Trade Union by paying up arrears of contributions, and emigration was also assisted where possible. Whatever its faults, the Society knew what it was talking about and its experience was a healthy antidote to the vague schemes of sentimental reformers. Other organizations playing a useful part were the Salvation Army and the Church Army, but their efforts were mainly concentrated, in practice if not in theory, on the more hopeless cases ; they were of little use to the more deserving victims, the unemployed artisans.

Davison tells the story of some relief workers in the year 1926 who found a tablet showing that the road on which they were working had been made by the unemployed in 1826. There seems to have been just the same controversies regarding the advisability of public works as a cure for unemployment as there were a hundred years later. In one of Macaulay's most famous essays—that dealing with Southey's Colloquies on Society—that arch-Whig uses the whole force of his invective to refute precisely the same arguments as have recently been advanced by his Liberal successors. " What is useful expenditure ?   ' A liberal expenditure in national works,' says Mr. Southey, ' is one of the surest means for promoting national prosperity.' What does he mean by national prosperity ?   Does he mean the wealth of the state ?   If so, his reasoning runs thus : The more wealth a state has the better ; for the more wealth a state has the more wealth it will have.   This is surely something like that fallacy, which is ungallantly termed a lady's reason. If by national prosperity he means the wealth of the people, of how gross a contradiction is Mr. Southey guilty. A people, he tells us, may be too rich : a government cannot : for a government can employ its riches in making the people richer. The wealth of the people is to be taken from them because they have too much, and laid out in works which will yield them more."

Macaulay was perhaps the greatest spokesman of the men of 1830. He had as little use for public works as for any other attempt to mitigate the rigours of *laissez-faire*. Apart from occasional out-relief given by the Guardians against task work in stone yards, and for the unsuccessful experiments in Ireland during the great famine, relief works seemed for many years to have been completely abandoned. After the fiasco of the Paris Ateliers Nationaux in 1848, in particular, probably every informed Englishman would have regarded them as dead and damned for ever.

But the cotton famine in Lancashire produced by the American Civil War was such an obvious case of undeserved unemployment that the Poor Law principles had to be relaxed. It took two years for Parliament to pay attention to the demand of the work-people that they should be employed not merely as a moral exercise, but for wages in works of public or private utility, but in June, 1863, an Act was passed authorizing the local authorities to raise loans for the new works.

The Lancashire experiment was practically the only successful instance of curing unemployment by public works during the whole century and it is particularly interesting to examine the methods used. It so happened that there was a great deal of obviously useful work to be done—road and street improvements, sewerage schemes and the like. The work was carried out on economic principles and the details were thoroughly attended to.   After a month's probationary training, the men were put on piece-work and encouraged to earn more than the minimum.   The inefficient were discharged, while the efficient were given regular employment.   The relief committees were wiser than their successors after the late war, and issued heavy boots and clothes suitable for wet and dirty work.   Although the scheme was limited in scope —there were never more than eight thousand workers employed—it provided a great many useful lessons. Above all, it showed that the provision of work for the unemployed could only be of value if it aimed less at mere relief than at the permanent rehabilitation of selected individuals.

Unfortunately these lessons were soon forgotten, and although repeated attempts to provide relief work were made during the depressions of the next forty years, the Lancashire principles were never once applied.   The standard rate of wages was not always paid ; instead of insisting on efficiency, individuals were merely expected to do as much as they seemed able to do—which had the natural tendency of reducing the general level of efficiency to that of the least competent worker ; the employment given was casual instead of continuous in order to spread it over as many people as possible, and the endeavour at any rate to apply partially the principle of " less eligibility " was enough to damn the schemes in the eyes of every self-respecting worker. Thus although schemes on these lines were greatly encouraged by Joseph Chamberlain's circular in 1886, they hardly ever attracted the decent worker for whom they were primarily meant but were merely added by the lowest classes of casual labourer to the list of temporary jobs by which they subsisted. It is not surprising that the schemes were regarded by workers in a cynical spirit well illustrated by the following conversation recorded by Davison between an enquirer and a relief worker engaged in digging up tree stumps in Hyde Park :

" When you have finished this job what will they give you ? "

" This'll take a long time, Guv'nor."

" Well, I suppose it will be finished sometime ? "

" Oh, then, I expect, they'll make us go and bottle off the Thames."

The next important measure after Chamberlain's circular was the Unemployed Workmen Act, 1905. It was an attempt on the part of the Conservative Government to regularize and extend a number of schemes which had been started by the Mansion House Charity Fund of 1903–4. That fund had established farm colonies in the country to which the heads of families were sent, while relief was given to their families in London. Similar colonies and other relief works were to be provided under the Bill throughout the country, and were placed under the administration of Distress Committees composed of representatives of the Poor Law, of the municipalities and of charity. Very optimistically the Act provided that the money for the relief works was to come from charitable sources ; in fact, of course, practically all the burden fell upon the rates. Provision was also made for assisted emigration, and there was some attempt at industrial transference. The principles under which the relief work was to be administered were not those of Lancashire, but a modified version of those laid down in the Chamberlain circular.   Except in so far as its administration gave for the first time an insight into the full scope of the problem, the Act was a complete failure.   In despair the harassed Conservatives, as one of their last actions, appointed a Royal Commission on the Poor Law whose report after three years' thorough investigation gave for the first time a practically complete survey of industrial insecurity.

Before considering this report, upon which all modern employment legislation is based, we must deal briefly with the most successful of all means of providing for involuntary unemployment—the insurance system developed by the workers themselves through their Trade Unions. The object of the Unions was not only to protect their members against destitution, but above all to protect their wage standards and their industrial status.   It is fatally easy for a craftsman to be forced by distress to abandon his craft and to apply for a job which throws him into the ranks of casual labourers. This cannot be sufficiently emphasized, particularly to those comfortable people who are sometimes heard inveighing against unemployed skilled workers who have refused to take on any poorly-paid casual labour that comes along.

Thus the Trade Unions were led to establish systems of out-of-work benefit, which by the end of the nineteenth century covered practically a million workers. As a rule there was a " waiting period " followed by a maximum number of weeks—about twenty on an average—for which benefit was paid. The Unions knew very well how to prevent malingering and they had devised an efficient system of registration.   Sometimes they gave travelling benefit to enable men to move about the country in search of employment, but more generally they relied on their own organization to find work. As the Unions became recognized by the employers as a necessary part of industry, the latter' often made a practice of applying to the Unions for the men they needed—for example, in the printing trade, this method of recruiting is still an almost invariable rule.

The report of the Poor Law Commission in 1909 was preceded by a full-length study of the whole problem by Sir William Beveridge. The title of the book was *Unemployment—A Problem of Industry*, by which the author meant that unemployment resulted rather from industrial fluctuations and casual methods of recruitment than from inherent defects in the men themselves. Personal defects to a certain extent determined the individuals who actually lost their jobs, but unemployment was inevitable for some, and the fact of unemployment reacted in turn on the men, making them less fit for employment.

Beveridge also stressed the importance of adjustment of the supply of labour to the demand. He showed how, in spite of the continual expansion of trade and industry and of the resulting demand for labour, unemployment had always persisted, even at the peaks of the recurring booms. The fact that unemployment had not increased as a whole in spite of the enormous expansion of the population showed that over-population was not a cause. Neither, on the other hand, was expansion of industry, however rapid, the solution. " Unemployment arises because, while the supply of labour grows steadily, the demand for labour,

c

in growing, varies incessantly in volume, distribution
and character. . . . It is obvious that, so long as the
industrial world is split up into separate groups of
producers—each group with a life of its own, and
growing or decaying in ceaseless attrition upon its
neighbours—there must be insecurity of employment.
. . . Unemployment, in other words, is to some extent
at least part of the price of industrial competition—part
of the waste without which there would be no competition at all. Socialist criticism of the existing order
has therefore on this side much justification." The
writer added that the answer to this criticism was that
there might be worse things in a community than
unemployment, and suggested that the practical
answer was to reduce the pain of unemployment to
relative insignificance—a task which he did not regard
as impossible.

The most important remedies he put forward were
the provision of maintenance through an insurance
system like those of the Trade Unions, and the
establishment of Labour Exchanges to render labour
more mobile and as far as possible to decasualize it.

When the Majority and Minority Reports of the
Poor Law Commissioners appeared it was found that
their diagnosis was much the same as that of
Beveridge's book. Moreover, it is rather difficult to
see why Minority members, who inclined to the left in
their sympathies and included Mrs. Sidney Webb, found
it necessary to present a full-length report of their own,
since the reports agreed not only on the facts but on a
good many of the proposed remedies.

In the first place they agreed in recognizing the
reality of involuntary unemployment. Employment

on reasonable terms was not always available even to the best workers, and it was thus impossible for the State to remain content with the deterrent Poor Law of 1834. The clearest classification of the unemployed was given by the Minority as follows :

(1) The Men from Permanent Situations, discharged by changes of process or the misfortunes of their particular employer or in industrial depressions.

(2) The Men of Discontinuous Employment, typified by those in building and other seasonal trades.

(3) The Under-employed, typified by the casual labourer at the docks and elsewhere.

(4) The Unemployables.

Both reports laid great stress on the practice of casual engagement of labour as a cause of under-employment, and the Majority made a special investigation of dock labour as the leading instance of casual employment and thus one of the greatest single causes of the production of pauperism and distress.

The Minority said practically the same thing. They reported that all their enquirers, starting on different lines of investigation and working independently all over the kingdom, " came without concert to the same conclusion, namely, that of all the causes or conditions predisposing to pauperism, the most potent, the most certain, and the most extensive in its operation was this method of employment in odd jobs."

The Minority, bolder than their colleagues, recommended drastic compulsory measures. They wanted the system of casual engagement done away with altogether and proposed to make it compulsory for all engagements of less than a month's duration to be made through a national system of Labour Exchanges.

A Labour Exchange system was also recommended by the Majority, although they did not recommend that it should be compulsory. Both reports insisted on the importance of proper education and training of juveniles, and strongly attacked the misuse of boy-labour in blind-alley employments. The Majority recommended an advisory organization for parents and boys in connection with the Labour Exchange, while the Minority proposed to prohibit any employment below the age of fifteen, and to have compulsory half-time work and education up to eighteen.

The possibility of counteracting business fluctuations by the giving of public employment was also mentioned in both reports. The Majority advised that Government Departments and Public Authorities should endeavour to undertake their irregular work when the general demand for labour was slack, while the Minority suggested a scheme—about which something is heard to-day—of a ten years' programme of public works to be used deliberately to counteract cyclical fluctuation.

Neither reports had a good word to say for relief works on the lines of the Chamberlain circular or the Unemployed Workmen Act, and both quoted with approval the same passage from two of their investigators : " The evidence we have collected seems conclusive that relief works are economically useless. Either ordinary work is undertaken, in which case it is merely forestalled, and later throws out of employment the men who are in the more or less regular employ of the councils, or else it is sham work which we believe

to be even more deteriorating than direct relief."
Finally both reports recommended a great extension
of unemployment insurance, the only difference being
that the Majority preferred a State system while the
Minority wanted a State subsidy to voluntary insurance
through Trade Unions.

The sole divergence of principle between the two
reports lay in their attitude to the old Poor Law.   The
Majority wanted on the whole to keep the Poor Law
together and to retain something of its deterrent spirit
for those not otherwise provided for under their recommendations.   The Minority recommended a new
Ministry of Labour which should be concerned not only
with measures for the prevention of distress through
unemployment, but with the problem of the distressed
able-bodied at all stages.   But even they recognized
the necessity of some deterrent for the work-shy, and
proposed, instead of the workhouse, maintenance of the
able-bodied " on condition that they submit themselves to the physical and mental training that they
may prove to require."   This training was to be given
to day-training depots or residential colonies, and for
those guilty of breaches of discipline a semi-penal
detention colony was to be established.

The substantial agreement of the two reports was
the more striking in view of the great difference in
outlook between the Majority and Minority members.
" From many different standpoints," writes Beveridge
in a subsequent work, " all the Commissioners had been
led by patient study of the facts irresistibly and almost
unconsciously to agreement;   through their own
enquiries, by the evidence put before them, through the
reports of their special investigators, they had come to

practically the same diagnosis and the same programme of principal reforms." Thus it was not surprising that the government of the day should have taken immediate action on the lines recommended, by establishing the national systems of Employment Exchanges and Unemployment Insurance.

I need make no apology for this rather lengthy analysis of Sir William Beveridge's book and the Reports of the Commission. For it is no exaggeration to say that, apart from a sporadic and comparatively unsuccessful revival of the old policy of relief works, there has been no substantial change in the policies then laid down, that no new method of handling the problem has been discovered. Regulations have succeeded regulations; laws have been passed and amended; special ministers (of Action and Thought) and special Commissioners have been appointed; but Employment Exchanges and Unemployment Insurance have remained the pillars, indeed the only effective instruments, of unemployment policy. The wisdom of 1909 remains the wisdom of 1936.

Had economic development since 1909 followed a normal course; had changes taken place gradually, with fairly regular alternations of boom and slump, as was the case during the nineteenth century, it may well be that the policies of 1909 would have proved adequate. But only five years later there began another of those great periods of transition and attendant dislocation which as we have seen have been among the major causes of catastrophic unemployment.

" We live," wrote Professor Robbins in 1933, " not

in the fourth but in the nineteenth year of the world crisis." Nobody looking at the world to-day, with its dictatorships and Totalitarian States, its struggles between Fascism and Communism, its revolutions and wars and rumours of wars, can doubt that the comparatively balanced pre-War political and economic system has given place to something far less stable. And the principal economic symptom of this is worldwide unemployment.

I do not mean to imply that we are to-day much worse off as a whole than before the War. On the contrary, wealth has increased and the standard of living has risen in this country and in many other parts of the world in spite of crisis. It is even probable that the War helped in this respect by the great stimulus it gave to technical improvements. Yet not only are we failing to make anything like the use we could make of this technical progress, but the dislocation and stresses of our system are greater than they have been since the Industrial Revolution, and possibly greater than those which accompanied the end of the Middle Ages or the Industrial Revolution itself.

This is not the place, nor have I the space, to give more than the briefest analysis of the chaotic period which was ushered in by the pistol-shots of Sarajevo. Quite apart from the sheer wastage of four years of destruction, the War left international trade wholly unbalanced and largely at a standstill ; the greater part of Europe was utterly impoverished ; industry had been forced by war production into a lopsided development quite unsuited to peaceful conditions, while vested interests sought at all costs to retain the value of the misdirected capital ; new nations endeavoured to found their sovereignty on the customs barriers ; while the financial and currency systems, the clinical thermometers of economic life, showed by their incredible inflationary fluctuations the deep-rooted diseases of the body politic.

Not until 1924 was a serious effort made to restore order out of chaos. The temporary settlement of the German Reparation problem—the best indication of the economic insanity of the period—ushered in the great attempt to rebuild the pre-War economic system whose tragic failure became widest in 1931.

Broadly speaking, the pre-War economic system was based on twin pillars. One was the gold standard, that is to say, a comparatively automatic international currency system. The other was relative freedom of trade and capital movement throughout the world. To restore these pillars was the declared aim of the leading figures in politics and business throughout the world.

But while the first pillar, the gold standard, was set up once more with comparative ease, neither the individual efforts of able and devoted men nor the resolutions of countless conferences and committees availed to restore freedom of trade. Thus the whole attempt at reconstruction remained lopsided, the gold standard could only be maintained by the temporary expedient of unbridled international borrowing, and eventually the whole structure collapsed.

Innumerable reasons have been put forward for this failure, despite the apparent agreement in principle achieved at conference after conference, to make any progress in restoring free trade, or even freer trade. The misguided enthusiasm of the new nationalities, the cupidity of vested interests, the obstinacy of the United States, the fallacious doctrines of self-sufficiency, the general state of insecurity and the desire to retain arms industries ; any of these and many other causes may have played their part. But at the root of them all may well have been a by no means blameworthy, perhaps largely instinctive, sense in the minds of governments, hinted at by Mr. Keynes in some remarkable articles in the *New Statesman* in 1933, that some kind of social control over economic development was essential, that not merely the interests of capitalists but the employment and thus the livelihood of their people could not conscientiously be left by statesmen to the ill-understood play of world economic forces.

All that can be said with certainty is that the crash of 1931 proved the methods of control to be wrong and the whole system unsound. We have to start again. Since the international method has failed hopelessly we must start at home. And we must start by concentrating on the problem which, as we have seen, lies right at the core of our troubled age—employment.

CHAPTER II

NOT long ago I told an acquaintance that I proposed to write a book about unemployment. " But surely," he said, " you are out of date. The problem is virtually solved. Business is on the up-grade everywhere and my difficulty is to get decent labour at all."

The remark was not surprising, although it would have sounded somewhat strange to my unemployed friends in Cumberland or Durham. Business conditions in Great Britain are not merely rapidly improving but have in many industries and districts developed into a real boom, while in some parts of the country the labour shortage is seriously hampering enterprise. And yet at any given moment over 1,600,000 people, or about 13 per cent. of the total of insured workers, are registered at the Labour Exchanges and in receipt of unemployment benefit.

It is true that this figure compares with about 2½ million at the worst stage of the slump. But if an employment situation of this kind is to be regarded as nothing out of the ordinary during a period which most of our newspapers unite in describing as one of remarkable prosperity, what are we to expect during the next slump ? The figures are still considerably worse than in the post-War years before the slump of 1930–31, years during which unemployment was universally regarded as far more serious than before the War. Yet it was before the War that Sir William Beveridge wrote :

" A great body of workmen to-day are men living on a quicksand, which at any moment may engulf individuals, which at uncertain intervals sinks for months or years below the sea surface altogether. Many of them, no doubt, become used to their place of habitation ; they have learnt its ways and continually escape destruction ; they might be unfit for any other life ; they have come there, perhaps, not by disaster but by their own weakness. Yet while this quicksand and its movements are part of industry, society cannot escape some responsibility for those who live there ; cannot treat as criminals those whose industrial services are there required ; cannot end the evil by rescuing individuals."

Society has admitted its responsibility. No longer do responsible men write, like St. Loe Strachey of *The Spectator*, that " a far more important factor than industrial disorganization is the moral disorganization caused by the belief that unemployment is not a man's fault, but his misfortune, and by the failure to realize that a man may have less evil done to him by experiencing for a time the actual pinch of want than by being pauperized at the hands of the State." Unemployment benefit exists ; it is sufficient to support life above the starvation line ; its stigma as a " dole " is no longer seriously felt. Beveridge's recommendation " to diminish the pain of unemployment " has been put into practice. But the quicksand of which he writes has been so vastly extended by the convulsions of a period of transition that society cannot rest content.

What is the extent of the quicksand in modern industrial life ?   Here the figure of 1,600,000 is of little use as a guide.   It merely represents the number of unemployed on the actual day the record is taken. But it is estimated that over five million different persons claim unemployment benefit or transitional payments in the course of a year.   In other words nearly half the total number of insured workers in Great Britain, including dependents perhaps 15 millions of our fellow-countrymen, have every year some personal experience of unemployment ; they have the fact of the quicksand forcibly brought to their attention. As Mr. J. A. Dale, of the Ministry of Labour, said in a paper read before the Royal Statistical Society to which I am largely indebted for the method of analysis in this chapter, this is a fact deserving of serious reflection.

The brighter reverse to this medal is, of course, that only a very small proportion of the five million get no work at all during the year, while the majority are only unemployed for much shorter periods.   As Mr. Dale points out, it is a complete—though a common—mistake to imagine that the monthly figure of those on the register represents a special class of unemployed industrial workers who are surplus to the needs of industry and permanently out of work.   For example, in August, 1936, only about 340,000 had been unemployed for a year or more, just over 400,000 for more than nine months, half a million for more than six months and about 650,000 for more than three months.   The majority of the remainder had been on the register for less than six weeks.

These figures do not, of course, indicate directly the most important feature of unemployment from the point of view of an unemployed man—the amount of unemployment he suffers during the year. Some of those, for example, who have been on the register for less than six weeks, may only have had a few weeks' employment during the year and may thus be suffering nearly as severely as those who have been out of work for the whole year. One way of estimating the numbers of those in this state is to look at the figures for persons claiming benefit without the thirty contributions qualification, that is to say persons who have had not more than 30 weeks' work during the past two years. They receive " unemployment allowances " as opposed to " insurance benefit," and totalled about 630,000 in August, 1936. Their numbers have fallen but little since the worst period of the slump. Although exact figures are not available, on a rough estimate a further 300,000—350,000 people will only just qualify for insurance benefit, getting on an average not more than four or five months' work in the year. Thus out of the five million odd people who come on the registers during the year, about a million are suffering really obstinate and prolonged unemployment.

As Mr. Dale points out, these people are really in quite a different category from the other four million, whose unemployment is intermittent. The intermittently unemployed include most of those recorded in the figures as " temporarily stopped " or " normally in casual employment " (about 300,000 and 70,000 respectively in August, 1936) as well as a considerable

number of those recorded as " wholly unemployed."
Some of these are short-time workers who, in a brief
period of a week or fortnight, are working part of the
time and " playing " the rest ; others are people who
have been " stood off " and have an understanding
that they are soon going back to work with their
previous employer ; while still others, recorded as
" wholly unemployed," while they have no such
expectation when they become unemployed, yet do
in fact return fairly soon to work. Thus the four
million (it will, of course, be obvious that this figure
has little relation with the published numbers of those
unemployed on a given day) slide gradually off towards
those whose severe and prolonged unemployment has
earned them the name of " hard core."

The " hard core " consists, as we have seen, of about
a million people who really are more or less " wholly
unemployed " in the popular sense of the words and
of whom nearly 350,000 get no work at all. It is not
a homogeneous collection of people, this million. It
comprises excellent workers who have had a long and
honourable record of employment ; and it includes
also those who have always had but a precarious
foothold in industry. One thing about them is
certain ; they are the really tragic sufferers from
unemployment, the men—and women—whose stories,
recorded in such books as Mr. John Newsom's *Out of
the Pit*, make such pitiful reading. Many of them have
had little or no work for years ; some not for a decade.
If the problem of the " hard core " could be solved, the
whole question of unemployment would take on quite
a different aspect.

A point to be noted in passing is that the very

existence of this "hard core" of more or less permanently unemployed has an important psychological reaction on those who are unemployed for much shorter periods. It greatly increases the general sense of insecurity. When a man falls out of work and his first efforts to get a job are unsuccessful, he begins to think—and he has plenty of time to think—of those of his mates, and others of whom he has heard, who have failed altogether in their search.   He thus tends to lose hope far more quickly than would otherwise be the case.

As Mr. Bakke points out in his remarkable book *The Unemployed Man*, this loss of hope and faith is one of the strongest reasons why Unemployment Insurance can never be, in the minds of the great majority of the nation's workers, a substitute for work.   With a job, even with a reasonable prospect of a job, the reason for living is secure.   Without it, it is gone. "Unemployment Insurance may partially make up the deficit in funds resulting from the loss of a job. It can never make up the deficit in broken minds and spirits."

Were there no "hard core," the general body of the unemployed would contain far fewer of these "broken minds and spirits."   For intermittent and casual employment, unsatisfactory though it is, Unemployment Insurance is a solution of sorts, a solution which "diminishes its pain."   But the "hard core" calls for fundamentally different treatment.

The more striking feature about the "hard core" is that it is very unevenly spread over the country. Very few members of it are found in the more prosperous, very many in the depressed areas.   Mr. Dale points out that this disparity has existed for years.   In 1926, of the 120,000 men drawing benefit without the contribution qualification, 50,000 were in the coal-mining industry. At the present time also this depressed industry, whose workers are among the finest in the country, accounts for a very large number in the " hard core," its unemployed living in isolated villages where there are few opportunities for work of other kinds. Ever since the War the applicants for outdoor relief have been largely concentrated in a few areas, three-quarters of these in 1930 being in 34 out of 631 old Poor Law Unions in England and Wales. The problem of the " hard core " and the problem of the depressed areas are largely one and the same thing.

This brief analysis corresponds roughly with another given from quite a different point of view by Sir William Beveridge in a recent lecture. He divided unemployment into four main categories : seasonal, interval, cyclical and structural.

The first two categories obviously fall into the class I have described as " intermittently unemployed." There are a large number of industries and trades in which employment is governed by the seasons. The best-known examples are agriculture, the building industry, the clothing trades (which are also subject to irregular fluctuations due to fashion), and hotel and boarding-house services at seaside and other resorts. Jam-making and herring-curing are other instances of work which must, in the nature of things, be done at certain seasons of the year. The motor and associated trades are partly seasonal. Even a section of the coal-mining industry, which is not generally thought of as a seasonal occupation, tends to be considerably more active in the winter than in the summer, owing to the increased demand for coal for domestic purposes.

In the past, the workers in these trades managed somehow to adapt themselves to the seasonal conditions, partly, as in the case of the building trades, by demanding and obtaining higher wages than those normally paid to more regular occupations. This, indeed, is a point noted by Adam Smith.

Thus the system of Unemployment Insurance has undoubtedly come to many of these workers as a boon, a real addition to their standard of living rendering it relatively tolerable. Certainly seasonal employment is not really satisfactory to those unable to obtain other work in the off-seasons. But while it can be mitigated by better organization (perhaps on the lines so well set out by Mr. C. T. Saunders in his book *Seasonal Variations in Employment*) it is clear that there is no fundamental cure within any economic system based on consumer demand. How, for example, are you to handle the employment problem of a Manchester mantle factory, instanced by Saunders, whose permanent staff is 30, whose average employment is 60, and whose maximum employment is 75 ?

" Interval " unemployment is the unemployment of people passing from one job to another, both often of a permanent nature. Here again it is obvious that Unemployment Insurance mitigates the pain of a transitional period inherent in any economic system, even that of Soviet Russia. The most that can be done is to endeavour, by maintaining industry and employment active and by instituting machinery to put workers " stood off " by one employer as rapidly as possible in

D

contact with another—the function of the **Employment Exchanges.**

In this classification Sir William Beveridge did not provide a separate heading for casual workers, whom in the first edition of his standard work *Unemployment —a Problem of Industry* he regarded as constituting one of the most serious problems of all. This is probably because he looks on them as included in the " seasonal " and " interval " categories, no doubt mainly in the latter. For after all a casual worker is mainly someone who is constantly passing from one job to another, with greater or less intervals. It is not the function of this book to attempt to indicate a solution for the immensely complicated problem of the casual worker, but it may well be that only the adequate provision of regular jobs and the general raising of standards will sufficiently diminish the supply of casual workers to force employers to abandon a method of odd-job employment which, as we have seen, the Royal Commission of 1906 describes as the most potent, the most certain and the most extensive in its operation of all the causes or conditions predisposing to pauperism.

With " cyclical " unemployment we come once again to the " hard core." I do not mean to imply that all the workers thrown out of their jobs by these recurring fluctuations of the trade cycle which have so exercised the minds of economists suffer really prolonged unemployment. But a very considerable proportion must in the nature of things remain unemployed for two or three years at least. Moreover, this particular kind of unemployment affects most gravely the skilled workers in the industries making " capital goods " (as opposed to consumption goods) such as machinery, shipbuilding, iron and steel and to a lesser extent coal-mining. These men are among the finest workers in the country and they are naturally, and rightly, extremely reluctant to abandon their own trade and run the risk of dropping into the ranks of the unskilled or casual workers. So they stay in their home towns and wait for their shop or yard or mine to reopen—in slump periods a search for work with other firms which are undergoing the same experience is, of course, fruitless. Such, for example, was for many years the lot of the men who built the *Queen Mary*.

The problem of cyclical unemployment is the problem of the trade cycle. No insurance or other palliatives can compensate a really skilled man for the suffering and hopelessness of waiting for years during which he feels his skill steadily slipping from him. Only positive measures for flattening out the trade cycle and maintaining a more regular flow of employment can be regarded as a satisfactory solution, and we shall see something of what the economists say on this subject in the next chapter.

" Structural " unemployment is the real basis of the " hard core." It includes all those affected by the great structural changes in industry which are one of the principal features of our age of transition. The cotton mill hands of Lancashire, displaced by Japanese and Indian competition ; the iron-ore miners of West Cumberland and the coal miners of Durham, Lanark-shire, Ayrshire and South Wales, many of whose mines can never be re-opened ; the shipyard workers of Clyde and Tyne whose only chance of permanent work is perpetual naval re-armament : most of these and many others, too, have lost their old employment for good.   For them, and for their children growing up in a hopeless atmosphere with no prospect of a job, Unemployment Insurance is no solution at all.   These are the men who people the " depressed " areas, and to put forward proposals for solving their problem is the principal aim of this book.

It is a great mistake to imagine that the whole problem of unemployment, or rather of employment, is contained in the monthly statistics.   Some important aspects are not touched by those statistics at all.

I am not referring here to the figures showing the number of persons relieved under the Poor Law. These figures are often quoted in the public discussions about unemployment.   They are well over a million, and it is often supposed, quite wrongly, that this million has to be added to the Ministry of Labour's figure.   In fact about half of these consist of persons not ordinarily engaged in some regular occupation, and their dependents—that is to say the " permanent poor " relieved on account of old age, sickness, widowhood and so on, and not on account of unemployment. Of the remaining half nearly all those eligible to be included in the Ministry of Labour statistics (that is to say the heads of households as opposed to the dependents) are in fact compelled to register at the Employment Exchanges and are thus covered by the Ministry figures.   Mr. Dale estimated that not more th n about 13,000 of those left out were able-bodied unemployed and could legitimately be added to the unemployment figures.   There is thus no question about these figures, and their reduction, being genuine ;

men have not been pushed off on to the Poor Law as has sometimes been suggested.

But in fact there are a good many people unemployed, and suffering severely, who do not register at the Employment Exchanges and are not eligible for insurance benefit. Most of these belong to one of the most pathetic of all the categories of unemployed—the unemployed " black-coated workers."

The Unemployment Insurance Acts draw a distinction between " manual " and " non-manual " workers. While all manual workers are insurable, whatever they earn, non-manual workers are only insurable if they are earning at a lower rate than £250 per annum. This means, of course, that, for example, a clerk earning £5 per week (£260 per annum) has, if he falls out of work, no other resource than the Poor Law. And no one with any understanding of the position and attitude of clerical workers, with their endless struggle to keep up appearances which indeed is expressed in their common designation of " black-coated worker," can doubt that only in the very last resort will they apply to the guardians or the Public Assistance Committees.

For many years the various organizations of non-manual workers—and they are a miscellaneous collection representing not merely clerks but journalists, architects, Correctors of the Press, coke oven managers, colliery under-managers, navigating officers, marine engineers, chemists, shop assistants, actors, musicians, theatrical employers, life assurance workers, and others —have been pressing for the removal or increase of the £250 limit, but without success. Not until 1935, four years after the slump had caused probably the biggest wave of dismissals of non-manual workers ever known, was the Unemployment Insurance Statutory Committee requested to consider the problem. Their report appeared in April, 1936, and they have recommended an increase in the limit to £400 per annum.

At the time of writing, action has not yet been taken. Indeed, in view of the facts that a minority of the Committee was opposed to the change, and that all the employers' organizations raised strong objections, it is perhaps not certain that action will be taken.   In that case the extraordinary situation will persist in which, for example, a shirt-cutter is allowed to be insured as a manual worker while a tailor's cutter, because he fits customers and designs patterns, has no such resource, or in which a typist who strikes the keys of a typewriter or a computor who strikes the keys of a calculating machine is placed at the same disadvantage as compared with a compositor striking the keys of a linotype or monotype machine. And an actor or variety artist who earns say £200 a year will still find himself excluded from insurance on the ground that his rate of earning when a show is running (without taking unpaid rehearsals into account) is greater than £4 16s 2d. per week.

If I may judge by my personal experience, in the shape of the numerous really tragic letters I received after a broadcast on this subject, I should say that the hardships and sufferings of many unemployed black-coated workers were even greater than those of their companions in misfortune among the manual workers. Standards of living are always relative, and there are few greater tragedies than those of good men seeing themselves and their families slipping down the social

scale through no fault of their own.   As we have seen,
they have no insurance to fall back on.   Moreover, it
is extraordinarily difficult for a black-coated worker,
particularly one nearing middle-age, to find a new job
once he has lost his old one.   The somewhat pathetic
name of one of the black-coated organizations—*The
Over forty-five Association*—is significant of this.   There
can be no doubt that a great many of the black-coated
unemployed belong to the " hard core."

But the numbers involved are, of course, small in
comparison with those of the manual workers.   It is
not easy to estimate them.   In 1934, the Trades Union
Council maintained that between 300,000 and 400,000
insured   and   uninsured   non-manual   workers   were
jobless.   Other guesses vary between that and about
150,000, and a rough calculation I tried to make from
the 1931 census returns indicated that the latter figure
was nearer the mark.

However, as this estimate includes the insured non-
manual unemployed it cannot, of course, be added to
the Ministry of Labour total.   For the number of
uninsured, the worst sufferers, we are dependent on
pure guesswork.   The Statutory Committee gives an
estimate by the Government Actuary which indicates
that the total number of salaried persons with incomes
between £250 and £400 a year is about 450,000.   If we
assume an unemployment percentage of 10 per cent.—
it seems generally agreed that the percentage in this
class is lower than among the manual workers—we reach
a figure of 45,000, and are probably erring on the side
of conservatism.

This may not sound very alarming.   But it should
not be forgotten that the importance of this middle-

class is greater than its relative numerical strength. That is one of the lessons to be learnt from the Totalitarian States, with which we shall deal at greater length farther on. The Nazi revolution in Germany in particular was largely made by a disgruntled, impoverished and insecure middle-class, by dismissed clerical workers, by university and secondary school graduates who could find nothing to do, by professional men who could barely scratch a living, by small tradesmen ruined by competition. Although the situation in this country is certainly not comparable with that in Germany, as the Statutory Committee points out in its report, the sense of insecurity has " spread into sections of the population who had hitherto felt themselves secure from unemployment." It is not without significance that University graduates, for whom prospects at the present time are relatively good (to judge from the replies I received from a question addressed to all British Universities), should have expressed themselves, in answer to a circular letter from Miss Eleanor Rathbone, M.P., overwhelmingly in favour of raising, indeed of abolishing, the insurance limit. Inadequate though an insurance benefit of thirty shillings or so a week must obviously be for men and women who may reasonably expect to earn up to £1,000 a year or over, they thought it well worth while to go to the expense and trouble of stamps and cards in order to secure the right to it.

We have reached a point when statistics will carry us no farther. We have surveyed roughly, but fairly comprehensively, the main categories into which unemployment may be divided. But the real subject of this book is employment.

Quite apart from the actual part of unemployment and its attendant sufferings, few people to-day would maintain that the existing social and political system succeeds in offering adequate outlets for energy and ability. There is everywhere a sense of frustration, well expressed by Mr. H. G. Wells in a recent series of articles in *The Spectator*, based on Steele's *Anatomy of Frustration*. We all feel, somehow, that modern science and technique is presenting us with a great opportunity, an opportunity for abolishing poverty and want, the eternal " pressure of population on the means of subsistence," the bitter struggle of humanity for its livelihood. We see prospects of increasing leisure for all, and its better use, of making a really civilized life available to the many instead of allowing it to remain the privilege of a few.

That is the real problem of employment. How can we so improve our system as to liberate latent human energies and abilities (the existence of which were so clearly demonstrated during the War) and direct them to these ends ? Let us see what the economic theorists have to say about our subject.

CHAPTER III

As we saw in Chapter I, the freedom of enterprise upon which nineteenth-century development and prosperity was based looked for its support to a great body of economic theory built up by Adam Smith and his successors, from Ricardo and Bentham to John Stuart Mill and Herbert Spencer. Generally summed up in the words of its first French exponents, " laissez-faire," the whole system rested upon the belief that to allow individuals to pursue their own material interests with the minimum of interference was the best way to secure economic progress. These " classical " economists were at pains to show that a mechanism of checks and balances and corrections, which despite its complications was of natural growth, ensured the proper working of the amazingly intricate system of exchange and production of goods throughout the world.

Although this body of theory was opposed to most previous economic theories and actions, notably those of the eighteenth-century Mercantilists against whom Adam Smith fought so protracted a battle, it held the field largely unchallenged through the century. Here and there advocates of tariff protection arose, such as Adam Mueller and Friedrich List in Germany— international free trade was never wholly accepted ; but the only really notable figure in opposition was Karl Marx.

I have not the space, nor does it fall within the scope of this book to attempt a detailed analysis, still less a refutation, of the Marxian doctrine. Nothing is more foolish than to underestimate the stature of the man whose writings are the real Bible for the population of one-sixth of the surface of the globe and for millions of men and women elsewhere. Nor is there a case for dismissing Marx as a serious economist and regarding him merely as the prophet of the proletariat. He used the theories of the classical economists and the doctrines of the most notable philosopher of the age, Hegel, to construct an intellectual case against the capitalist economic system which, as we shall see, is still capable of serious defence—and attack. But since Marx, although he lived and wrote in England, has had until recent years extraordinarily little direct influence upon English thought, I shall confine myself to discussing the theories of the modern neo-Marxists later in this chapter.

As Miss Gertrude Williams points out in her excellent book *The State and the Standard of Living*, the attack on *laissez-faire* in Great Britain was social rather than theoretical in origin. The " New Trade Unionism " of the eighties, although it had abandoned the more or less unquestioned acceptance of the capitalist system which characterized the founders of the movement, was still a rather vague demand for a new scale of values, for a world which upheld the dignity of the common man, for what Tom Mann and Ben Tillett described as " a co-operative commonwealth to be reached by effort in various directions." William

Morris was a great dreamer, and although H. M. Hyndman began to interpret the Marxian doctrines and to emphasize the regulative function of the State, the fact that the most influential moulders of Socialist thought, the Fabians, started out with the vaguest of sentiments and only gradually began to build up a loose body of theory is surely sufficient evidence that British nineteenth-century Socialism was essentially non-doctrinaire.

None the less, towards the end of the century the clear and logical Benthamist teaching that *laissez-faire* invariably meant " the greatest happiness of the greatest possible number " had been partially undermined and serious theoretical opponents of the classical teaching began to appear.

The chief point of attack was the most vulnerable feature of capitalism, the recurrent crises and subsequent depressions, which as we have seen are among the most important causes of unemployment. There must surely be something wrong with a system which every decade or so threw millions of men out of work through no fault of their own, which allowed valuable buildings to fall into disuse, machinery to rust and unsold goods urgently needed by starving people to rot or be thrown away.

To explain this blot on their system the capitalist economists advanced a number of explanations. One of the most curious of these was the sun-spot theory of Professor W. S. Jevons, who maintained that the periodical sun-spot fluctuations affected the weather, and thus the harvests, and thus the whole course of economic activity. But since the depressions were irregular   and   the   sun-spot   fluctuations   regular obviously this would not do. Other economists, the forerunners of the monetary theorists of to-day, emphasized variations in the quantity of metallic currency available, due to gold discoveries and so on ; while still others laid stress on misdirection of productive energy, or the mistakes of manufacturers in forecasting the demand for their goods.

One of the most important of the early contributors to the subject was on the attacking side—Mr. J. A. Hobson. He was the first man to put forward a logical and easily understandable theory of under-consumption.

Hobson maintained that the inequitable division of wealth between rich and poor was the chief cause of trouble. While the workers have but the bare necessaries for existence, the wealthy classes—the capitalists—have more than they can possibly spend. Since they cannot spend their money they must needs save it, and they can only save by investing in fresh factories and means of production. While the factories are being built all goes well and there is plenty of employment, but the production soon outruns the demand. The market is glutted ; factories have to close down ; and the familiar cycle of depression and unemployment sets in. The root of the disease, in fact, is " over-saving," or from another point of view " under-consumption." The only radical remedy is to spend more and save less, which can only be done by redistributing income in favour of the workers, who spend the bulk of their wages, and at the expense of the wealthier classes, who will thus be unable to save so much.

For all its limitations, which were particularly

clearly pointed out in Sir William Beveridge's first book, this theory has had a great influence on economic thought.   Obviously it provided an excellent basis for Left-Wing criticism of the existing order, particularly of the distribution of wealth.   It was a powerful argument for raising wages—the remedy invariably advocated by Trade Unionists for depression and unemployment—as well as for the taxation of high incomes.   And its twin tenets, under-consumption and over-saving, remain important features not merely of most modern Socialist and neo-Marxian thought, but of the theories of many non-Socialist economists as well.

Since Mr. Hobson put forward these views, shortly after the turn of the century, a very extensive literature has grown up around the problem of the trade cycle and it may be said to have become one of the most important departments of economics.   Modern theories on the subject can most conveniently be divided into three main groups—those of the monetary theorists and currency reformers, those of their capitalist opponents, and those of the Socialists and neo-Marxists.

The first group covers an extraordinarily wide range. At one end are the extreme currency reformers, sometimes unkindly known as the currency cranks.   Broadly speaking, they base their arguments on the fact that periods of depression invariably have as their principal characteristic an obvious deficiency of purchasing power.   People are unable to purchase the goods they have produced.   To purchase them they need money. The trouble must therefore evidently be that there is a shortage of money.

By far the best known extremist is Major Douglas,

who is not merely a currency theorist but the leader of a politico-economic movement which has spread throughout the English-speaking world. The advocates of " Social Credit " have recently secured power in the Canadian province of Alberta, and seem to be becoming increasingly influential in Australasia, notably in Tasmania and New Zealand. Some of them even have shirts of a distinctive colour, which I believe is green.

Douglas maintains that he has discovered a fundamental flaw in the capitalist system of distributing purchasing power. He was led to make this discovery during his early experience as an engineer—a class incidentally which always resents the financial control exercised by the business side of an enterprise. He noticed one day that the " costs " of his factory's production were considerably greater than the amounts paid out for wages, salaries and dividends. Assuming that the same thing held good for other factories, he reasoned that this must surely indicate that the cost or purchase price of the total volume of goods produced was always greater than the total volume of purchasing power or money issued to consumers to purchase them. The remedy, therefore, must be to issue more purchasing power, which Douglas proposed to do in the form of National Dividends for all.

This argument is best known as the A + B theorem of Social Credit, which divides factory costs into A — those which are distributed as purchasing power in the form of wages, salaries and dividends, and B — those which are not so available, notably the charge for " depreciation." In its original form the A + B theorem completely neglected the obvious fact that

the " depreciation " costs represented renewals and
repairs of buildings and plant, and ultimately reached
the consumer as wages, salaries and dividends paid
out by the concern undertaking the repairs or providing
the new renewal plant.   Although the theorem has
been considerably modified to meet this objection, it
has not yet succeeded in convincing any serious
professional economist.

Social Credit is but one of many extreme currency
theories, whose popularity has always varied according
to the degree of prosperity at the time.   And all these
theories have had as one of their principal objects the
discrediting of the banking system and the gold
standard upon which it was based.   Supporting the
bimetallist theorists of the nineties, William Jennings
Bryan thundered his denunciations of those who
" crucified humanity on a cross of gold " ;   while the
more modern reformers have their disciples who
believe international Jewish bankers to be responsible
for the world's ills, and can call upon the services of
earnest dreamers like the late A. R. Orage, or Mr.
McNair Wilson, who endeavoured to show in *Monarchy
and Money Power* that it was the " Money Power " of
the financiers which throughout history had thwarted
the efforts of statesmen and patriot kings to secure
prosperity for the people.

It is easy to sneer at the currency extremists and to
call them cranks ; it is not difficult to refute most of their
theories.   But none the less, the course of events, and
even the evolution of economic thought, have
undoubtedly run in the direction which they sensed,
however vaguely and illogically.   The gold standard
has broken down and the greater part of the world's

trade is carried on without it ; while to-day probably the majority of economists, at any rate of Anglo-Saxon economists, agree in attributing the trade cycle of boom and slump largely to monetary causes.

The most noteworthy pioneer in this development was Mr. R. G. Hawtrey. The central feature of Mr. Hawtrey's theory is best described in his own words as " the inherent instability of credit." Although this phrase sounds rather formidable its meaning is in fact very simple.

It is generally understood nowadays, even by the most unversed layman, that the term " purchasing power " does not merely cover the metallic money and currency notes we carry in our pockets. The vast majority of payments to-day are made without using coins or notes at all, namely by drawing cheques on our banking accounts. Thus bank deposits, representing the ability to draw cheques, are just as much a part of our " purchasing power," indeed of our money, as coins and notes. They are in fact " bank money," and if anything happens to diminish their aggregate volume the purchasing power available to purchase the goods we have produced is also diminished.

What influences the volume of bank deposits, of " bank money " ? Not merely, as even bankers have sometimes suggested, the amount of money deposited at the banks, for that in its turn is dependent on other factors. The governing influence is the amount of credit granted by the banks, whether in the form of loans, overdrafts or investments. To go into the details of the argument, now universally accepted, would take too long ; but its kernel is not difficult to understand. The credits granted and investments

E

made by the banks are their assets, which must equal their liabilities (their deposits). Thus anything which influences the amount of credits and investments granted by the banks must also influence the deposits, or " bank money " available.

Business depressions are almost invariably ushered in by financial crises (such as that of 1931) which must be carefully distinguished from the depressions themselves. These crises occur at the end of a boom period when business men have been competing among themselves to borrow and invest thus forcing up interest rates and prices. Suddenly the bankers get frightened. They see their liabilities growing (as a result of their increasing loans) while their reserves, which are dependent on the note-issue and the policy of the Central Bank, remain the same, or may even be diminished as the result of the Central Bank's having in its turn been rendered nervous by gold withdrawals, or for other reasons. So the bankers begin to call in their loans. This diminishes " bank money " and thus purchasing power. Buying falls off. Then the business men in their turn get frightened. They sell stocks of goods on the markets and stocks and shares on the Stock Exchanges. Prices fall rapidly. Finally the public get frightened. Rumours get about concerning the solvency of banks. There may be a " run " on a bank leading to failure. The crisis is in full swing.

The crisis leads to a depression. Gradually the banks regain their " liquidity," their customary relationship of cash reserves and liabilities. They stop calling in loans ; they may even be anxious to lend. But the nervous state of business in general continues and business men refuse to borrow. Indeed

why should they borrow ?   Buying is at such a low
ebb that traders see no prospect of prices rising (and so
do not increase their stocks of goods), while manufacturers see no reason to put up more factories when
they cannot sell the output of those they already have.
Credit, and thus the available amount of "bank
money " remains " contracted."   Above all, the total
volume of investments remains far lower than it was
before the crash.

This is the point where Mr. J. M. Keynes steps in.   I
do not propose, nor have I the space, to follow him
through the closely-reasoned and intricate argument
of *A Treatise on Money*.   To make the logical—and
mathematical—steps of that argument clear to the
general reader is certainly a task beyond my powers.
It will perhaps be sufficient to say that the
argument has not yet been seriously refuted and
that many able economists both here and abroad
regard Keynes's claim to have discovered a serious
logical flaw in the monetary side of the self-acting
mechanism of the capitalist system, and particularly
in its dogmas of " sound finance," as expounded by the
classical economists from Adam Smith to Marshall, to
be definitely established.   In any case we must be
content with a brief analysis of the most important
feature—the function of investment.

Mr. Keynes maintains that variations in the volume
of investment are the principal cause of economic
fluctuations, so that if the volume of investment can
be controlled the problem presented by those economic
fluctuations can be mastered.   In contradistinction to
many of his colleagues he presents his solution in a
comparatively simple form, as a course of action which

presents no serious difficulty to a modern government, at any rate not to one of a wealthy State.

We followed Mr. Hawtrey's analysis of the financial aspect of the trade cycle up to the point when business men could not see profitable reasons for borrowing and opportunities for investment. Now the national income, the flow of purchasing power to individuals in the form of wages, salaries, interest, dividends and profits, is partly spent on ordinary consumption and partly " saved." The normal function of savings is to finance enterprise. Business men, or limited companies—the " entrepreneurs " of economic terminology—borrow the savings of the public directly through the medium of shares and debentures, indirectly through bank loans, and invest them in the construction of factories, in the purchase of machinery and merchandise and so on. As long as they are doing this to an extent sufficient to absorb the available savings, all is well. But as soon as a depression causes them to cease doing it the savings part of the flow of purchasing power coming from the economic system is not fully used to purchase the goods produced. Some of it remains idle in the banks and elsewhere. There is thus a real deficiency of purchasing power which tends to accentuate the depression, to produce a still greater reluctance to borrow and invest, setting up the vicious circle with which we are so tragically familiar.

Here once more is the " over-saving " of Mr. Hobson, although the analysis is different. So is the remedy proposed.

Mr. Keynes does not advocate, like Mr. Hobson, taking action to diminish savings by, in a modern phrase, "soaking the rich"; he wants to attack the problem from the other end. How can borrowing and investment be stimulated to an extent sufficient to absorb savings and thus secure a balanced flow of purchasing power and goods?

In a capitalist system it is not possible to compel business men to invest. But in a modern State investment by private enterprise is not the only way savings can be absorbed and converted into purchasing power. The State, and public authorities (such as municipalities) under its control or influence, can also borrow and spend the money on public works of national importance. If they do this during a depression to an extent sufficient to make up for the deficiency of private business investment the flow of purchasing power will again balance the flow of goods. The vicious circle will be checked. Prices will begin to rise and optimism to revive. Gradually private business investment itself will pick up, and as it does so the State can, of course, afford to diminish its borrowing and spending until eventually the ship of private enterprise is proceeding smoothly under its own steam.

The initiated will be able to point to many gaps in this brief description of one of the most brilliant—and promising—of modern economic theories, notably to my failure to refer to the influence of foreign trade and to my very sketchy description of the rôle of bank credit. But I think the real meat of the theory is there. As it stands, it is, of course, by no means entirely new. Public works as a cure for depression and unemployment are as we saw in the first chapter at least a century old. The new feature is the closely-reasoned theoretical basis for their function and above all the emphasis on the fact that they must be paid for by borrowing, that they must consist of what Mr. Keynes calls " loan-expenditure."

The public works which Macaulay derided in his attack on Southey, as well as most of the futile relief works of the nineteenth century, were mainly direct attempts to create employment and were paid for out of taxation. If there was one dogma which British nineteenth-century governments held fanatically, it was the dogma of " sound finance." Public expenditure—for relief works or any other purpose— must balance public income.

There was only one exception to this rule—war. The most respectable government might borrow to its heart's content for destruction, but to increase the National Debt for constructive purposes was the financial sin of sins.

To attribute this doctrine chiefly to nineteenth-century governments is unfair ; it is still widely held to-day. In his pamphlet " The Means to Prosperity," a reprint of some remarkable articles printed in *The Times*, during March, 1933, Mr. Keynes directed the full force of his reasoning powers towards proving that public loan-expenditure was calculated, by breaking the vicious circle of depression and thus increasing the national income as a whole, to improve public finances rather than to worsen them. He showed that the failure of the public works policy of the Labour Government was not due to any inherent fallacy in the reasoning but to the catastrophic decline in exports, and a consequent deterioration in the foreign balance of payments which caused far more unemployment that was directly and indirectly created by the loan-expenditure on public works. And he pointed out that the remarkably efficient conversion policy of the Bank of England and the Treasury had, by reducing the rate of interest to an exceedingly low level, created highly favourable conditions in which the long-term cost of the loan-expenditure he advocated was far lower than it had been before.

None the less he failed to carry conviction with the National Government. No one without full inside knowledge of the discussions within Cabinet, Treasury and Bank of England can pretend to give all the reasons for this decision, made in the face of a very considerable body of public opinion in the country. But I believe that some indication is to be found in a certain divergence of views between Mr. Keynes and Mr. Hawtrey, who as one of the economic advisers to the Treasury is more representative of official opinion.

While Mr. Keynes pins his faith on the gradual effect of Government or Government-influenced loan-expenditure towards increasing the general volume of spending, Mr. Hawtrey advocates giving the economic machine a sharp and sudden impulse calculated to revive optimism and induce business men to resume investment. The best illustration of this method is to be found in the actual course of economic development in Great Britain since the crises of 1931.

Since we left the gold standard, British economic life has received two impulses of the type envisaged by Mr. Hawtrey. The first impulse was the depreciation of sterling and the resulting check to the fall of wholesale sterling prices, and the second impulse was the introduction of tariffs, which gave British manufacturers an immediate advantage over foreign competitors as well as influencing prices in a similar direction. These two impulses stopped the rot, and, in conjunction with the well-managed reduction in the rate of interest, gave the necessary impetus to the business recovery we are now experiencing.

The National Government may have been right in the circumstances of the time. But as Mr. Keynes and others have pointed out there are limits to this policy. The depreciation of the currency is a device which can only be used sparingly and which, moreover, is apt to have an adverse effect on the trade of foreign countries, which are thus provoked to reprisals. Much the same is true of the tariff method. While a free trade country can secure the needed impulse by putting on tariffs ; once those tariffs are an established part of the economic system they cannot be indefinitely increased. Thus the methods by means of which we have got industry going again are in a sense " non-recurring," and, moreover, give some ground for the complaint of many foreign countries that we have stimulated recovery at their expense. These methods will not be available, or at least will not be so effective, in the next depression, so that it is obviously advisable to seek alternatives.

Another reason for Mr. Keynes's failure to get his policy adopted may be that its advocates are largely confined to Liberal and moderate Left-Wing economists and politicians, while even his diagnosis is not so widely accepted among economists as that of Mr. Hawtrey. Even so cautious an economist as Sir William Beveridge writes of the central feature of the Hawtrey theory—the " inherent instability of credit "—as " one of the recent assured advances of economic science."

Many economists of standing, like Mr. D. H. Robertson, Mr. J. R. Bellerby, the German Professor Schumpeter, and Professor Cassell of Sweden, to mention only a few, have been working on similar lines, while even Professor Pigou, one of the chief modern critics of the monetary theory of the trade cycle, is by no means wholly in opposition. The report of the Macmillan Committee on Finance and Industry, drawn up by a very widely representative selection of economists, bankers and business men, was largely based on the monetary theory.

The real fount and origin of the widespread research into the monetary aspect of the trade cycle is the desire to find some practical method of controlling and thus preventing the catastrophic fluctuations of the economic machine. But during the last few years another school of economists has come forward maintaining that the only way to prevent those fluctuations is to exercise no control at all. The motto of this school is in effect " Back to Bentham."

The head and founder of the school is an Austrian economist, Professor Mises ; hence it is generally known as the Viennese School. Its chief exponents in this country are Dr. Hayek, a Hungarian domiciled in London, and Professor Robbins, both influential figures at the London School of Economics.

According to Dr. Hayek and Professor Robbins the economic troubles of the post-war world are due, apart from the destruction and dislocating influence of the War itself, simply and solely to the misguided attempts of politicians and economists, bankers, business men and trade unionists, to interfere with the self-acting mechanism of economic life. Had it not been for tariffs and quotas, subsidies and bounties, rigid trade union wage rates, and efforts to bolster-up prices, and above all for monetary management—cheap money policies, open market purchases of Central Banks, Government borrowing for public works, currency manipulation and depreciation ; had we in fact followed the doctrines of classical orthodoxy with an austere disregard of immediate consequences, unknown since the seventies, we should have long since achieved that perfect equilibrium of the capitalist system which alone can lead to economic salvation and prosperity.

One of the most interesting features of this neo-Benthamism is its analysis of the trade cycle, ably stated in Dr. Hayek's *Money, Credit and Prices*. Here again it would take us too far afield to follow Dr. Hayek through the intricacies of his argument. But broadly speaking, he maintains that the trouble with the economic system to-day is not that too little money, too little purchasing power is available, but that we have too much money, or rather too much credit.

For slumps, he argues, are but the consequences of the foregoing booms ; while booms in their turn are the result of an excessive expansion of credit. Dr. Hayek more or less accepts the Hawtrey analysis of the function of credit and its inherent instability. He points out that the free granting of credit leads (as we have seen) to an increase of " bank money " and hence of purchasing power, which induces business men to borrow still further to meet the rising demand for their goods until ultimately the whole structure collapses.

His attack on the bankers for lending too much is so powerful that one cannot help feeling that he would prefer all transactions to be carried out on a purely cash, or metallic coinage basis, since this could not be expanded except by the slow process of mining, but the remedy he in fact advocates is the return to a rigidly orthodox gold standard and a severe restriction of credit as soon as any outflow of gold shows that expansion is under way. Both he and Professor Robbins maintain, for example, in contradiction to most British economists, that the chief blame for the collapse of 1931, rests not on the American and French authorities for "sterilizing" the gold they absorb, but on the Bank of England for not drawing the proper conclusions from its weak gold position and restricting credit irrespective of the effect on British trade and employment.

There is no mistaking the logical strength of the case put forward by the Viennese School, of which I fear I have only been able to give the vaguest idea. But there is also no mistaking its essential ruthlessness.

Not very long ago I heard a young English exponent of these views holding forth on the economic value of starvation. The main obstacle to recovery, he said, was the rigidity of wage levels due to the influence of the Trade Unions. Only by smashing the Trade Unions could we restore the free individual bargaining in the labour market which alone could lead to a " natural " wage level and thus to economic equilibrium and prosperity. And only widespread starvation could destroy the Trade Union movement.

Quid esset demonstrandum ; the logic is clear. But

could any modern State conceivably carry out such a policy ?   Indeed, quite apart from the question of Trade Union wages, could any modern State conceivably abandon, in the face of the fundamental Socialist attack on the capitalist system, all the mechanism for securing some sort of control over our economic life which has been evolved not merely since the War but during the last half-century ?   Surely the answer to Dr. Hayek and his friends is a simple *non possumus ?*   Right or wrong, the die is cast ; we cannot travel that way.

It is not difficult, however, to see the opportunity which the Viennese School's condemnation of any departure from the strictest Benthamism presents to the extreme exponents of Socialist thought.   Just as Marx based his great denunciation of the capitalist system on the theories of the classical economists, so the modern neo-Marxists find in the ultra-classical doctrines of Dr. Hayek and Professor Robbins the most solid support for their renewed attack.

The best illustration of this is Mr. John Strachey's book, *The Nature of Capitalist Crisis.*   I do not know whether Mr. Strachey is generally recognized as a serious economist.   He is certainly not a professional economist, and I am told that he is indebted for much of his thinking to other Communist theorists such as Mr. Palme Dutt.   But I have rarely read anything to equal, for sustained brilliance of apparently logical reasoning, the comprehensive review of the capitalist system and its economic thought with which Mr. Strachey leads his readers irresistibly to the conclusion that the Master was right all the time.

The main thesis of the book is, of course, that the capitalist system, the system under which the primary motive-power of the economic machine, the influence governing the decisions of the individual business men and corporate enterprises (limited companies, etc.) who control production and distribution, is private profit, is sick unto death. Whatever functions it may have been called upon to fulfil in the past, the system has irrevocably entered its " period of decline," foreseen by Marx eighty years ago. That is the real reason for our crises and depressions, our wars and threats and rumours of wars.

Mr. Strachey surveys the struggles of " declining capitalism," its unemployment, its frustration, its poverty in plenty. In a sweeping survey, to which I am quite frankly indebted for suggesting the method of presenting this chapter, he passes in review the proposals of the economists for patching up the decayed and tattered system. Major Douglas is right ; there is a fundamental flaw in the mechanism, but it is not the flaw which the apostles of Social Credit indicate. Nor is it a flaw which can be remedied by any monetary manipulation or currency reform, by any planning or control or attempt to flatten out the trade cycle. One by one the theories put forward to such ends—perhaps significantly with the important exception of that of Mr. Keynes—are faithfully dealt with.

They are dealt with by the weapons provided by Professor Robbins and Dr. Hayek. Indeed, Mr. Strachey goes farther. He does not merely use Dr. Hayek to destroy his colleagues, he does not content himself with pointing out the impossibility of putting the Viennese School's remedy into force ; he actually employs Dr. Hayek's analysis to demonstrate the truth of the Marxian doctrine.

To do this he uses chiefly a feature of Dr. Hayek's theory to which I have not yet referred, and to which I can only refer briefly now. Dr. Hayek employs a conception which he calls " lengthening the structure of production." He is referring to a well-known aspect of economic evolution, the increase in the number of different processes which take place before articles are brought on the market—the blacksmith had simply to make a hoe and sell it, but now somebody makes a machine to make the hoe and somebody else a machine to turn out the handle and other people make the machines to make the machines to make the handle and the hoe.

Dr. Hayek believes that if the smooth course of economic development is to be maintained, this process should not be interfered with by an excessive flow of purchasing power into the " consumers' goods " department as opposed to the " producers' goods " department. If there is an excessive demand for the produce of the machines, there will be a tendency to draw away capital and labour from making the machines, and a game of pull devil pull baker between the makers of the machines and the users of the machines to make articles of consumption will ensue, with a consequent rise of prices—anathema to Dr. Hayek—and eventual inflation.

Mr. Strachey argues from this that capitalism can only function by eternally and increasingly making machines to make machines to make machines, in other words by putting more and more effort into " lengthening the structure of production " and less into producing the consumption goods which the people need. This, he says, is absurd.

The argument is sometimes put in another way. The object of capitalism, it is held, is " accumulation." Everybody who can do so strives to "make a fortune," to accumulate capital or to add to that already accumulated in order to ensure security, or freedom from the impelling necessity to toil, for themselves and their descendants. This has the same result as that suggested by Dr. Hayek and satirized by Mr. Strachey ; it diverts an increasing proportion of the flow of purchasing power from the purchase of consumption goods—food, clothing, housing, necessities and luxuries —to the purchase of, or investment in, factories and plant and machines for whose production no market can be found. Readers will recognize the affinity with the " over-saving " theory of Mr. J. A. Hobson.

These are perhaps the most important arguments of modern neo-Marxian Socialism. They can be traced back to Marx, albeit not always very easily. They appear in many forms, but the essence of them all is the contention that the fundamental problems of employment, production, and distribution, of poverty in plenty, of liberating human energies for the satisfaction of human needs, can only be solved by the complete abandonment of the motives of individual profit and accumulation, by the transference of all the main decisions regarding production to a central planning agency, in fact by a comprehensive and whole-hearted change of system. For Mr. Strachey and those who think like him the sin of sins is to advocate half-way houses, as do moderate Socialist theorists like Mr. G. D. H. Cole, Miss Barbara Wootton in *Plan or*

No Plan, and many others. It must be all or nothing.

You pays your money and you takes your choice. I have endeavoured to give a bird's-eye view of some of the best-known cures advocated by our economic doctors to-day. It is true that many important theories, many important names, have had to be left out altogether. But none the less I think there is a not unrepresentative choice of cures—or nostrums—and I can only refer readers who wish for further information to the orginal works.

It may be objected that I am not playing the game by concluding the chapter without indicating my own particular nostrum. But the study of economic theory always leaves one appalled by the amazing complexity of the subject. I read one well-constructed and logical piece of argument and am deeply impressed ; I read another which tends in precisely the opposite direction and am equally impressed.

Perhaps my theoretical qualifications are insufficient. But I often wonder all the same whether economic science can be said to have the same solid basis as other sciences, as the physical sciences in particular. It deals so much with an intangible and almost incalculable factor—the nature and motives of man.

Let us assume, however, that economics, or, as it used more accurately to be called, " political economy," is a science. If there is one salient characteristic of the method by which science has progressed to its astounding modern achievements, it is the thorough use of practical experiment.

It is not easy to make experiments in political economy. The livelihoods, and even the lives, of human beings are at stake. We may feel that that rules out experiments which involve the complete reversal of existing methods and means of livelihood, at any rate until the more moderate cures have been properly tried out. But does it absolve us from the duty of making use of one of the few really sure means of progress mankind has yet discovered ? Can we afford to shrink from experiment in economic life, even from bold experiment, with an employment situation such as we have been studying ? And if we admit that we cannot, what direction should our experiment take ?

It is perhaps not wise to try to answer these questions on a basis of theory alone. Let us first take a look at some of the most far-reaching experiments in the world around us—those of the Totalitarian States.

F

CHAPTER IV

LESSONS FROM THE TOTALITARIAN STATES

WHATEVER opinions we may hold about it there can be
little doubt that the Totalitarian State is the outstanding discovery of modern politics.   It is not merely
based upon a complete reversal of all the tenets of that
great " liberal " movement which, beginning with the
" enlightenment " of the eighteenth century, seemed to
have established itself so securely, at any rate as an
ideal, in the years before the War ; it has not much in
common with the absolute monarchies, military
dictatorships and other tyrannies of the past.

For the Totalitarian State is not merely anti-liberal,
anti-democratic ; it is also democratic.   It destroys all
the   slowly   evolved,   or   theoretically   designed,
mechanism to ensure government of the people, by the
people for the people.   But it does not neglect the
people.   On the contrary it makes far more energetic
and determined efforts than any other form of State in
history has ever made to secure the wholehearted
support of all its citizens.

In the brilliant defence of the totalitarian principle
contained in the preface to *On the Rocks*, Bernard Shaw
points out that the citizens of Soviet Russia live under a
régime of " unlimited liability."   Whereas the citizens
of a " liberal " State are free to act as they wish within

certain known limits and are only punished if they actually transgress the law, those under a totalitarian régime enjoy no such security. They are expected to give their active allegiance and support to the Dictatorship of the Proletariat, to National-Socialist Germany or to Fascist Italy as the case may be. If they do not —and they can never be certain what action or omission, what whispered sentence or half-spoken thought will be construed as a want of allegiance— retribution may overtake them. " My movement," said Hitler in an interesting published dialogue with the poet Hans Jost, " conceives Germany as a corporation, as a single organism. Within this organic entity there is no irresponsibility, no single cell which is not responsible with its existence for the progress and good of the community. In my philosophy there is no room whatever for the ' unpolitical ' person."

Since every member of a Totalitarian State is expected not merely to obey, as the subjects of all but the most bigoted of autocrats were expected to obey in the past, but to co-operate wholeheartedly under the direction of the Leader in the national effort, it becomes a matter of vital importance to inspire them all with an essential unity of purpose, a common *Weltanschauung* or philosophy. Whether it is Marxian Communism, as interpreted in Stalin's periodical pronouncements on the " general line " of " the Party," or the Aryan " folk community " as expounded in *Mein Kampf*, or the imperial destiny of Fascist Italy ; all must accept the faith, and woe betide the heretic whose words or actions are calculated to undermine it.

This totalitarian claim on the individual is not really political at all ; it is essentially religious, and here perhaps is the real explanation of G.B.S.'s contention that a little unlimited liability would do the comfortable people of Great Britain no harm.

For as Mr. Keynes so wittily remarked in the *New Statesman*, apropos of G.B.S.'s comments on H. G. Wells's interview with Stalin, Shaw was the Divinity master of his generation, just as Wells was the Stinks master. Wells was disappointed in the technical and economic achievements of the Soviets, but Shaw was impressed by the faith, by the spirit of sacrifice, by the Spartan living he saw around him. And Keynes went on to suggest that the young men and women who visited Russia and returned to this country so full of enthusiasm were in the same case. They were enthusiastic and happy not because they found prosperity and its comfortable fruits, but because they found extreme discomfort. Satiated by the civilization of Oxford and London, to see and experience Spartan living in alliance with faith so impressed them that they were prepared to overlook all the squalor and misery and cruelty which is not so far away even from the conducted members of an Intourist party.

It is that faith, held not merely by the Communist Party but by the great mass of the working classes, which has carried Soviet Russia through the tragedy, the devastation, the appalling privations of revolution, civil war, and the period of " War Communism," when over two million people were killed quite apart from those who died of starvation ; that faith strengthened the Russian people to support the immense sacrifices called for by the first Five Year Plan ; and that faith is little if at all dimmed to-day. It is many years since I was in Russia, but I shall never forget the spirit of the young Communists with whom I used to go boating in Leningrad in 1924.

That is the first great lesson to be learnt from the Totalitarian States—for it is by no means confined to Russia. Hitler has won the German masses by giving them something to believe in—a conclusion confirmed recently in the *New Statesman* by no less a person than Mr. R. H. S. Crossman, who as an active Socialist can hardly be suspected of excessive sympathy with Naziism. And Mussolini seems to have done much the same thing. The supreme value of faith, the practical demonstration of the deep-seated longing of men and women in a supposedly sceptical age for an inspiration which can only be described as religious, are subjects upon which we should do well to ponder.

I am, I fear, a rather sentimental person, particularly susceptible to the influence of flags, bands, community marching and singing, indeed to all the devices employed since time immemorial to foster mass enthusiasm. In the early days of the Nazi Revolution in Germany, while engaged in the by no means excessively simple task of trying to understand and interpret it, I must confess to having fallen an easy victim to Dr. Goebbels' skilful methods of suggestion. I have rarely enjoyed an evening so much as one spent with the eager Nazis of Schöneberg, in Berlin, celebrating the unveiling of a memorial to Schlageter, the German ex-officer shot by the French for sabotage in the Ruhr. We marched in a torchlight procession to salute the Minister of Propaganda ; we attended a memorial service ; we sang endless inspiring marching songs ; and finally we consumed endless quantities of beer and corn brandy while settling in animated conversation the affairs of the universe.

The stage management was excellent, but in spite of my susceptibility I do not think it was that alone which captured me. It was even more the community spirit, the sense of comradeship between all classes, the genuine attempt to establish a new sense of social equality which is expressed in the Nazi phrase *Volksgemeinschaft*—" folk community."

A considerable part of Hitler's *Mein Kampf* is devoted to drawing conclusions from his principal political axiom—that the fount and origin of all power in a modern State is to be found in the broad masses of the people. If you can once win the people, there is no need to bother with the upper strata, and above all with the " intellectuals." They will have to fall into line. Moreover, since the people as a whole are the vital factor, it is essential to do away as far as is humanly possible with class distinctions, with the barriers between the " masses " and the more highly-educated classes. If the latter wish to play their part, particularly if they wish to lead, they must do so through intimate contact with and knowledge of the people, not with any thought of privilege or superiority but on a basis of fundamental equality.

Such is the theory. The practice may not always come up to it. But none the less, whatever the fallacies, distortions and cruelties of National Socialism it is a real mass movement. And few who have seen the labour camps and other institutions of the New Germany where rich and poor, university graduate and board school boy, are brought together in the equalitarian atmosphere of camp and barrack life, would deny that a genuine and wholehearted effort is being made to carry out the Führer's ideas.

Communists in Soviet Russia and elsewhere would, of course, pour scorn on the possibility of any such development. They would say, and they do say, that the labour camps are a barefaced attempt to delude the masses. Class is merely a question of cash, and as long as you have rich and poor, capitalists and workers, an attempt to create a " folk community " is completely ridiculous.

Yet in Soviet Russia to-day very considerable differences of income and privilege are developing, and the methods by which they are being rendered palatable to the less fortunate among the Soviet masses are not so very different from those employed in Germany. The Soviet Union may still be in a preliminary state of transition towards the Communist ideal, but it affords none the less practical proof that the community spirit depends more on moral and social than on absolute economic equality. The annihilated or rather " liquidated " bourgeoisie has given place to another, but as in Germany the greatest possible efforts are being made to maintain close contact between it and the masses of the people.

The recent developments in Russia seem to show that a " bourgeoisie " or middle class is an essential feature even of a collectively organized modern society. And the importance of the middle class is perhaps the most outstanding lesson of the tragic developments leading to the establishment of the various Totalitarian States.

Few more vivid historical pen-pictures than that in

Trotzky's *History of the Russian Revolution* have ever been painted. The utter futility of the Tsar and his entourage, the corruption and inefficiency of the great bureaucracy, the complete disintegration of the ruling classes, the disastrous state of the army, particularly of its leadership, the terrible privations suffered by the peasantry and the working classes ; all is brilliantly delineated by the masterly brush-strokes of Lenin's great collaborator. But the most salient feature of the Russia of 1917 is the almost complete absence of a middle class.

Throughout the illimitable countryside landowning nobles faced land-hungry peasants ; in the towns Trotzky notes that the lateness of Russian industrial development had led to industry and even trade being established on a large-scale pattern by a few great capitalists or foreign concerns, so that there, too, the wealthy few faced the poverty-stricken many. The War, with its attendant corruption and profiteering, had tended still further to increase this disparity. There were plenty of talkative intellectuals, but nowhere was to be found anything approaching the solid phalanx of small and middling tenant or landowning farmers, owners or managers of little businesses, clerks, accountants and executives of manufacturing and trading concerns, retired men and shareholders with a modest competence, which characterizes every great modern industrial state.

Thus the supporters of a Liberal Republic from Miliukov to Kerensky had no real backing. There was no dam to stop the radical flood which swept so rapidly through the masses and led them to be far more forward in demanding measures of expropriation than were the

Bolsheviks themselves—a point Trotzky particularly stresses.

Yet had it not been for the genius of Lenin, for his careful preparations and organization, his wisdom in holding back the workers in the " July days " and choosing the precise moment to strike in October, and above all perhaps for the fatal policy of the Liberals in carrying on the war and thus further embittering a suffering army which wanted to get home, there might never have been a Communist revolution in Russia. Moreover, after the revolution had taken place the resistance put up by the upper and middle classes, aided it is true from abroad, necessitated the slaughter of millions before the work of liquidating the bourgeoisie was complete. Assuredly a Communist experiment is not easy to begin.

The failure of the Left in Germany points much the same moral as its success in Russia. I have always held the view that the usual criticism of the unfortunate German Social Democrats was based on a fundamental misapprehension. It is suggested that in 1918 they should have pursued a genuinely revolutionary policy and rejected the co-operation of the generals, the permanent officials, the business men and other erstwhile supporters of the old order. They would then certainly have been forced to co-operate with the extremists in a policy of wholesale confiscation.

This would have rallied the whole of the upper and middle classes, together with a peasantry incomparably better off than that in Russia, against the proletarian revolution. Indeed this is what actually happened in Bavaria and Hungary, when the revolution was comparatively easily submerged by a violent and victorious reaction. The Berlin Social Democrats at any rate succeeded in maintaining a strong position for the fourteen years of the Weimar Republic.

But while their realization of the strength of the middle classes was one of the principal motives behind this moderation, the course of events during the Weimar Republic compelled the Social Democrats to make their bargains with the great capitalists. Economic pressure caused the middle classes to be crushed between the upper millstone of large-scale capitalism and the nether millstone of Social Democracy. Above all their savings were swallowed up in the most catastrophic inflation known to history.

It was among these ruined and embittered middle classes that the seed of Hitlerism grew to strength. The growth passed comparatively unnoticed during the years of fictitious and borrowed prosperity before the great depression. But from 1930 onwards, when their jobs began to disappear as rapidly as their savings had vanished seven years before, the middle and, above all, the lower middle classes, flocked in millions to the Swastika banner. They were the people who carried Hitler into power ; the working classes were not won till later.

It may be suggested that there is a contradiction between these two conclusions—that the Totalitarian States show the vital importance on the one hand of the masses as a whole, and on the other hand of the middle classes. But in the first place the smaller group shades off very gradually into the larger ; there are infinite gradations between the wealthy industrialist or land-owner and the completely property-less " proletarian " —gradations for which little or no place is to be found in Marxian theory. And in the second place the political importance of the middle classes only becomes overwhelming when a fundamental threat to their existence and ideals rouses them to take violent action. Above all at those crucial moments when the bullet becomes the chief political argument, the middle classes enjoy the supreme advantage not of bravery, for there have been few braver men in history than workers on the barricades, but of being able to muster in their ranks the vast majority of those with gifts of leadership, knowledge of military science, and control of the military machine.

Thus as long as the middle classes are carried along in a political movement which does not threaten completely to overwhelm them, as long as their standards of living are not excessively undermined, the real political weight remains with the masses. Here again Nazi Germany affords an illustration ; despite the fact that National Socialism was originally a middle-class movement the process of merging the middle class in the masses is going on inexorably all the time. There are different ways of achieving the " classless State."

This is a book dealing primarily with an economic subject, and it may be felt that I have wasted quite enough space on political digressions and that it is time I endeavoured to deal with the economic aspects of the great totalitarian experiments. But the political digressions were perhaps not quite irrelevant and certainly the foregoing argument must be held to have some bearing on the possibility of trying out Mr. Strachey's whole-hog remedy.

However, it is unfair to rule out an economic thesis on purely political grounds. The Marxian doctrine has been put into practice in Soviet Russia.   What are the results ?

Here it will no doubt be objected that Russia in her backward state has not yet been able to put real Communism into practice at all.   She is still merely in the preliminary stage of State Socialism.   But enthusiasts for the Soviet system like the Webbs make a great point of the fact that the fundamental principles of Socialism as opposed to Capitalism—the elimination of the accumulative motive and the central planning of all decisions regarding production—are fully enforced.   And surely after nearly twenty years during which economic theory has been supported by an almost unparalleled religious enthusiasm and by the extreme political ruthlessness which characterizes the Totalitarian State, the Soviets must be prepared to see their economic achievements judged on their economic merits.

The political passions and partisanship aroused by the Soviet system are so intense that it is extraordinarily difficult to reach any impartial conclusion regarding its economic achievements.   Not having been in Russia since 1924, I have no personal experience to put forward and statistics are notoriously misleading.   But recently one of the most highly-respected and fair-minded personalities in the British Labour movement has visited Russia for the express purpose of discovering the truth on this point.

In a lecture, whose report appeared in *The Times* on the day I write these lines, Sir Walter Citrine said that Russia had surmounted in the main her most pressing economic problems.   The question most people asked was whether the system worked, and he thought no fair-minded person could say that Russia had made no progress. There was economic progress on all sides. There was building going on everywhere. The standard of craftsmanship was low, but it should be remembered that it was difficult to improvise a vast army of workpeople taken from the peasantry and to put them on to construction work. Nevertheless, some of the architecture was outstanding, and in industrial buildings Russia was in possession to-day of some of the finest equipment in any part of the world.

Labour conditions were in many respects in advance of those in other countries. It was true that the standard of living was deplorably low when compared with Western countries, but the real comparison should be with the conditions under the Tsarist régime. Housing was still very congested. It was the rule, rather than the exception, for the Russian worker and his family to be confined to a single room. The growth in population was enormous, and so far from overcoming the housing problem Russia was falling behind.

Sir Walter does not really help us to reach a conclusion. Russia has undoubtedly progressed, particularly when the comparison is made with conditions under the Tsars. But is the progress more or less than it would have been under an efficient capitalist system ?

Mr. H. R. Knickerbocker, one of the best-known and most fair-minded American journalists in Europe, conducted not long ago an investigation into relative standards of living in Soviet Russia and in the capitalist border states which had formed part of the old Russian Empire, a comparison which he maintained was as fair as any such comparison could be. He eschewed statistics in the study and went direct to the kitchen. In conversation with housewives he found out what people ate (and not merely what they ate in general but what they were going to have for dinner), when they went to the cinema, how much tobacco they smoked, what they drank and so on. After progressing in this way all along the Western and North-Western Soviet border, on both sides of the frontier, he reached, I think somewhat reluctantly, the conclusion that the capitalist States won every time.

I do not suggest that we should accept Mr. Knickerbocker's view or Sir Walter Citrine's view or, indeed, any of the countless conflicting views or opinions or articles or books which deal with this difficult problem. I merely suggest that we should suspend judgment. The Soviets' claim to have solved the problem of plenty is not yet established.

Another claim, on which particular stress is laid in the Webbs' monumental work on *Soviet Communism*, is that Russia has solved the problem of employment. There are no unemployed, they tell us, in the Soviet Union.

Certainly there are practically no officially admitted unemployed ; there is no system of unemployment insurance. But the claim is by no means fully recognized by opponents of the régime. Moreover, the tremendous capital investment of the Five Years' Plan, taking place as it did in a backward country where industrial workers only formed a small proportion of the total, largely peasant, population, obviously created an insatiable demand for labour. What the position will be when Russia is as fully industrialized as Western countries remains to be seen.

None the less, Russia undoubtedly possesses the

great advantage over capitalist countries that she can
exercise social control over industrial development.
She may have some " seasonal " unemployment ; she
almost certainly has " interval " unemployment.   But
she seems to be able to take the necessary measures for
avoiding " cyclical " and " structural " unemployment.
Although the new insistence on accounting, on making
enterprises pay for themselves within a more normal
financial system, may eventually be found to restrict
the activities of the Central Planning Bureau, there is
no likelihood of enterprise being left entirely to
individual industrialists actuated solely by the profit
motive.   The Government can always speed up capital
investment and start new industries when it seems
advisable.   The value of this is one of the most
important lessons to be learnt from the economic aspect
of the great Russian experiment.

The claim to have found the method of dealing with
unemployment is not confined to Soviet Russia ; it is
also made by Nazi Germany.

When Hitler assumed power in February, 1933, over
six million Germans were registered as unemployed.
Nearly a third of the whole people was dependent upon
doles of one form or another.   This proportion was
worse than that of any important country with the
possible exception of the United States.

The devastating effect of this unemployment upon
the people, and above all upon their morale, is not
difficult to imagine.   The system which gave them
bread had broken down and they waited, uncompre-
hending.   The leaders of business and finance, the
orthodox economists, even the Trade Union leaders,
offered no remedy ; they said that nothing could be

done but tighten belts and wait for the crisis to end as other crises had ended.

The methods by which the unfortunate Dr. Brüning sought to master the situation would have brought joy to the hearts of Professor Robbins and Dr. Hayek. A conversation I had the privilege of having with the ex-Chancellor just after the Nazi revolution convinced me, if further conviction was needed, that he held to one economic dogma—sound finance, and that he had one supreme fear—inflation. With the unbending persistence of a fanatic he stuck to the gold standard till the whole banking system crashed about him ; with the sternness of a man to whom self-denial was the essence of religion he forced wage and salary reductions till the Trade Unions and Social Democrats had lost their hold on the workers. But he never caught the electric hare of financial stability ; he merely per-petually diminished the volume of spending, investment and employment.

The most vivid expression of the deep-seated yearn-ing for a fundamental change of policy which carried the Nazis into power was contained in a speech by the ill-fated Gregor Strasser not long before his tragic fall.

" The rise of the Nazi movement," he said, " is the protest of the people against a State which denies the right to work and cannot restore a natural means of livelihood. If the distributive apparatus of the economic system in the modern world does not under-stand how properly to distribute the bounties of nature, then the system is wrong and must be altered. . . . The important feature of the present situation is the great anti-capitalistic yearning which is going through our people, which already possesses, consciously or unconsciously, ninety-five per cent. of our people. This anti-capitalistic yearning is not in the least a rejection of property morally justified by its origin in work and savings. . . . It is the protest of a people against a degenerate economy, and it demands from the State that it shall, in order to ensure its own right to live, break with the demons of Gold, World Economy, Materialism, with thought in terms of export statistics and Reichsbank discount rates, and secure honourable remuneration for honourable labour."

The industrious German people demanded the right to honourable labour at all costs. And whatever we may think of the Hitler Government and its methods, it has not been unsuccessful in this respect. The six million unemployed have at the time of writing been reduced to little over a million, and although the statistics are sometimes alleged to be cooked, the cooking is certainly not very serious.

The Nazis tried out nearly every possible and impossible method which has been suggested for dealing with unemployment. They settled large numbers on the land ; they pushed women out of industry by steady pressure combined with a bribe in the shape of a marriage dowry and replaced them by men ; they forced businesses to engage unwanted staff ; they endeavoured to " spread " available work by reducing hours ; they looked askance at labour-saving devices and favoured the processes which employed the most labour. But by far the greater part of their success has been secured by two main lines of policy. The first is financial in its nature and has obvious affinities with that advocated by Mr. Keynes.

From the moment when the Nazis came to power the

G

volume of " loan-expenditure " was steadily increased. The Government borrowed money—at first from the banks, later from the public, and spent it on direct and assisted public works, or subsidizing private investment, and later on an unparalleled programme of rearmament. The results were as foreseen by Mr. Keynes. The volume of spending increased, gradually private investment began to pick up, and eventually a very considerable industrial revival was generated.

The second method is more revolutionary. Broadly speaking, it consists in influencing and indeed largely controlling the activities of private enterprise, the actions of property-owners, instead of expropriating them.

The first essential, as we have seen, was to induce them to invest. So subsidies were granted for investment ; for example, in order to absorb the unemployed in the building trade during the winter off-season, householders who renovated their properties or subdivided them into small flats received a proportion of the cost from the State. Tax reduction was also utilized to the same end—profits spent by businesses on renewals and fixed capital investments were, in fact, exempted from tax altogether.

Such methods were naturally not unwelcome to business men, but sterner measures were to come. It is said that Frederick William I, who did much more than his son Frederick the Great to lay the foundations of Prussian greatness, had a habit of walking about the towns in his domain. When he saw a particularly prosperous-looking burgher he would call him aside, point to a suitable piece of ground, and remark laconically, " *Er baut hier ein Haus* " (you will build a house here). Protestations were unavailing ; the burgher had to build his house, and for the rest of his life he probably had to work harder than he liked to keep it up. This way of stimulating industrial activity may well have afforded the model for Dr. Schacht, who is said often to deal with recalcitrant industrialists by offering them the choice between voluntary action and action under compulsion. The various campaigns of the Nazi Party are, of course, another effective method of exerting moral influence on property-owners—it is distinctly unwise not to stand well with the Party authorities. In particular, the organization of industry for war production has been carried out by completely dictatorial means ; Hitler had only to issue a few orders to convert the peaceful town of Dessau into a vast factory for military aeroplanes, working day and night.

The German Totalitarian State has not merely evolved a technique for directing economic effort into the channels where its rulers consider that effort to be needed, and for absorbing the technically unemployed ; it has succeeded in mobilizing much of the immense energy latent in the German people. The semi-voluntary activities of Hitler youth, Storm Troops, and the many other group formations of the Nazi Party, the compulsory labour camps for young men—and young women—and above all the armed forces and their auxiliary organizations ; all serve this end. And the tragedy is that so much of this energy, ability and effort, inspired as we have seen by a genuinely religious enthusiasm, is directed towards preparation for war.

The concentration on rearmament and military organization is perhaps the main reason why, in spite of the absorption of the unemployed, in spite of this great mobilization of purposeful effort, the standard of living of the German people as a whole has risen little if at all. " Real wages," the purchasing power of individual employed workers, has certainly declined, largely as a result of a rise of prices which the controlling mechanism of the State has failed to avert. Here and there an actual shortage of certain commodities, notably fats and meat, has made itself felt.

Another reason for this is, of course, the precarious international economic position of Germany. A policy of expanding internal purchasing power within a country tends to increase imports and diminish exports. While wealthy nations can do this for some time without ill effects (*cf.*, America under Roosevelt) and may even find that they are so stimulating world trade that a balance at a higher level can ultimately be achieved, a poor country with few reserves is soon brought up short. That is the real cause of the foreign trade restrictions and barter methods which Dr. Schacht in his " New Plan " has developed to a pitch challenging comparison with the Russian Amtorg. Only the rigid control of foreign trade could ensure the most efficacious distribution of the limited amount of foodstuffs and raw material Germany can purchase with her exports and prevent the import of all but the most essential foreign products.

Finally, it may be that we see here the limitations of a policy of public works, military expansion and unproductive investment generally. To a certain extent it seems evident that " loan-expenditure," whatever its object, will induce economic revival, but beyond a certain point adverse effects on living standards begin to show themselves. Italy (which

I hesitate to discuss for want of direct personal knowledge) surely affords evidence that great public works
and magnificent roads are not synonymous with
prosperity ; the contemplation of the most sumptuous
buildings is a poor cure for an ill-filled stomach.

This brief survey of the Totalitarian States and of
some of the lessons to be learnt from their experience
is not written in any spirit of admiration of their
principles. I do not believe with Bernard Shaw that
the modern State must maintain its faith and its unity
in the same way in which the mediæval Catholic Church
sought to do so, that is to say by exterminating or
" liquidating "—wonderful and expressive word—
heretics or the socially incompatible. I yield to no
one in the conviction that the methods of free discussion
and representative government, which our people in
particular have slowly evolved through the centuries,
constitute for the community a real step forward in the
advance of civilization and for the individual a prime
essential of a good, useful and happy life.

But it is above all from the Totalitarian States that
we can learn something about the elemental forces
which are stirring in the modern world. For great
peoples as for individuals adversity is always the
supreme test. The underlying stresses and strains of
our civilization are largely hidden in western countries
by layers of comparative comfort—and of comfortable
people ; in nations which, like Germany and Russia
and to a much less extent Italy, have been through the
uttermost depths they lie on the surface plain to see.

We have touched on the problem of class warfare and
two possible ways of solving it ; we have seen the

supreme importance, at any rate in the opinion of men who have shown by their success that they had their fingers on the pulse of mankind, of maintaining the confidence of the masses of ordinary people in their leadership and system of government ; we have learnt what unemployment can do to political stability and considered some experiments in dealing with it.   Above all we have seen the longing for faith, for something or somebody to believe in, for a vital leadership which calls for the active co-operation of all.

Why should that longing be confined to Russia or to Germany or to Italy ?   Is it not far more probable that it is slumbering elsewhere, waiting for the touch of a leader or, it may be, of a charlatan, to awaken ? Unless the free countries of the world find means to awaken it while retaining their freedom it may be awakened by men to whom freedom is but something to be extinguished with a firing-squad.   This may be a book on an economic subject, but if true this con- clusion surely has some bearing on the question we asked at the end of the last chapter—whether we should be prepared for bold experiment.

The last great lesson to be learnt from the Totalitarian States we have mentioned as yet only indirectly.   It is the remarkable fragility of the veneer of civilization upon the primitive emotions of mankind.   Many of the same decent sort of men who in England would be busily improving their bowling action or getting down to scratch may have been instruments of the Terror against the Trotzkyists in Russia, or have competed for places, not in a club or college team but in the firing squads of the S.S. guards during the great " purge " of June 30th, 1934, in Germany.   And as I write many others are ruthlessly murdering unarmed political opponents in Spain.

It is, of course, possible to dismiss these happenings with a shrug of the shoulders, to say that nothing of the kind could happen here. But a most disturbing doubt remains in my mind whether similar conditions of economic pressure and domestic strife would not produce similar results, even in England. Once the binding force of tradition is gone, once questions are at issue on which men feel too deeply to leave them to the counting of heads or to rational discussion, once political passions are thoroughly stirred up, these things are possible and may be inevitable.

May not this also have some bearing on our economic discussion? If we are to make bold economic experiments, surely it is wisest to endeavour to make them in a direction which commands the maximum of common agreement and arouses the minimum of political animosity. What should that direction be?

CHAPTER V

THE DEPRESSED AREAS—TRAGEDY

FROM the first green on the Seascale Golf Course—or
rather links, for it is a genuine seaside links—is visible
one of the most lovely and varied panoramas in the
British Isles. To the east, beyond the downlike foot-
hills, lie the mountains—Scawfell, Scawfell Pike, the
Screes, Lingmell, Great Gable, Kirk Fell, and the rest
of them ; to the north-west on a clear day the hills of
Galloway tower beyond the Solway Firth ; to the west
the Isle of Man rises out of the sea ; while in exceptional
weather, so they say, you can see Ireland, 80 miles or
so away. If ever the Psalmist's words were true, they
should be true here ; you have only to lift up your eyes
unto those hills to feel the strength which emanates
from them. The air is so full of life that it is a call to
action in itself.

And yet West Cumberland, a district as favoured by
Nature as any in Great Britain for scenery, climate, and
natural wealth, has been in the grip of intense depression
ever since the War. Only seven miles from Seascale,
at Egremont, the long line of derelict mining villages
begins, where over 10,000 good men are eating their
hearts out in idleness, and, what is far worse, losing
little by little the capacity for work if it should come.
If we drive along the endless straggling streets of

88

Cleator, Cleator Moor, Frizington and Arlecdon, we shall hardly see a single smiling face, only little groups of men, and women, too, hanging about at every street corner with soured, hopeless expressions.

Turning west to Whitehaven, where the management of royalty owner and lessors has led to the closing of the great mines upon which the prosperity of the town depends, we may find less squalor, perhaps, but equal depression and hopelessness. Over fifty per cent. of the male population are unemployed. Farther north, in Workington, things are a little better ; but Maryport, again, has over fifty per cent. of unemployment, and the isolated mining villages beyond, where the mine has closed for ever, are in an even worse case.

We drive on through the comparatively prosperous town of Carlisle and over the lovely Pennine moors towards the North-East Coast. We can make short detours, perhaps, to Alston and Haltwhistle, little isolated pockets of unemployment round about the fifty per cent. mark. And so on to the Tyne.

I think it was Tyneside which first made me realize what a depressed area was. Imagine a vast straggling town stretching for miles along the river banks, inhabited by nearly a million people. Once we have passed through Newcastle proper (which retains some prosperity as the county town), we shall hardly see a single decent house. Row upon row the shabby dwellings crowd one upon the other. Here and there the gaunt steelwork of a derelict shipyard or the chimney of a disused factory, or the dingy grey mountain which indicates where a coalmine has been, breaks the sky-line, but there is scarcely a tree to give shade or add a touch of colour to the landscape.

Tyneside affords a classic instance of the segregation of the poor. Coming in from the west we shall have missed the single wealthy residential suburb of Gosforth and we drive for miles and miles through a bewildering number of separate boroughs—the " balkanized " local government of Tyneside is a serious problem in itself—inhabited almost solely by the working class. A recent census showed that in Hebburn, out of a population of some 24,000, there were less than 50 persons belonging to the employing class ; and there were no professional men except the doctors and clergymen whose work compelled them to reside in the town.

From Hebburn we pass imperceptibly into Jarrow, whose population of 30,000 souls depended almost entirely on a single vast enterprise, Palmer's shipyard, which under the shipbuilding nationalization scheme cannot be reopened for forty years. Here the unemployment is not unnaturally well over 50 per cent., and while elsewhere the percentage is better, and is improving with the recovery in the staple industry of shipbuilding, there are still over 70,000 unemployed " workers " on the Tyne.

Driving south through the Durham coalfield we find a different landscape but the same problem. Here once more are innumerable mining towns and villages where the mine will never be worked again. We can visit Witton Park and Woodside, where out of a total population of 2,600 some 670 persons, or practically every soul available for work, is on the live register, and nearly half of them are drawing neither Unemployment Benefit nor Transitional Payments. In the village of Leasingthorn, with a population of some 600, we shall find that the annual cost of Transitional payments and

Public Assistance is nearly £10,000, 98 per cent. of those on the live register having ceased to be eligible for Unemployment Insurance, while if we want to make a concentrated study of the " Hard Core," we can go to Butterknowle, where 32 per cent. of the many unemployed have been out of work for more than five years.

Thus in a morning's run in a fast car we can cover a pretty representative selection of the tragic " Special Areas " in our green and pleasant land. We shall have left out the Scottish area round the Clyde and the valleys of South Wales, but we should only find much the same sort of thing there. We can perhaps use our imagination to visualize those, and the other depressed areas, such as North-East Lancashire, which are not quite bad enough to be officially scheduled. If we are busy in the prosperous South we may not be able to spare very long, but we can fortify ourselves with a round of golf in the loveliest district in England and I think we shall find the trip worth making.

Out of a total insured population of just under a million in the scheduled Special Areas of England and Wales, over 300,000 are registered as unemployed. That represents a proportion of over 30 per cent. The proportion of unemployment for the whole of Great Britain is under 13 per cent.

Our motor trip will perhaps have given us some idea of what this means. But we shall hardly have had time to make a close investigation of family circumstances.

In any study of the effects of unemployment it is essential to remember that the real unit is the family. Probably the vast majority of working-class families, even of families living together and thus constituting a household, have more than one member of working age ; very often there are several. In a relatively prosperous area it is most unlikely that all or even the majority will be out of work at the same time. While the advantage which this gives is to some extent diminished by the much-disputed Means Test, it none the less goes a good way towards mitigating the moral and material effects of unemployment.

Moreover, in this connection it is worth noting that in districts where, as is the case throughout the developing industrial areas of the Midlands and the South, industry is widely diversified, an increasing variety of opportunities are open to the members of each family. Father may have lost his job for good ; he may perhaps have had the misfortune to be engaged in a type of employment which is tending to disappear, such as horse-van driving or clog-making, or even one which has vanished altogether like crossing-sweeping. But his sons may be carving out careers as motor or aeroplane or radio engineers, in the electrical trade, with traffic-signal manufacturers or in a cinema, while his daughters get work in a beauty-parlour or hairdresser's shop, or in one of the many modern light industries where female labour is so greatly in demand.

In the depressed areas, on the other hand, such opportunities are few and far between. Many families have all their members out of work. Moreover, owing to the fact that the areas have so largely depended upon one or two " heavy " industries such as coalmining or shipbuilding, women and girls have remained at home and the number of earners per family has been small. In the issue of *Planning*, dated October 8th, 1935, this point is particularly stressed.

Planning compares the situation in Oldham and Rhondda. The population of Oldham is given by the 1931 census as 140,000 and that of Rhondda as a thousand more. At the same time unemployment in Rhondda was returned as 13,500, while in Oldham it was above 18,500, so that to all appearances Oldham was the more heavily hit. But while Rhondda had only just over 42,000 workers in employment, Oldham had still nearly 63,000. A worker's average earnings would therefore have had to be about a third lower in Oldham than in Rhondda in order to pull it down to the same level of poverty, whereas in fact earnings in Oldham were probably the higher of the two.

The broadsheet goes on to point out that the average of workers in employment per family in England and Wales in 1931 was 1·63, or for employed and unemployed together 1·84. But while East Ham had 1·7 persons per family in employment, Rhondda had only 1·22. If all the unemployed in Rhondda had had jobs, the number and proportion of wage-earners supporting Rhondda families would still not have caught up the East Ham level, even though East Ham had to carry 6,000 unemployed.

Here is an important reason why a given rate of unemployment hits the heavy industrial depressed areas much harder than other districts. Another important reason is also connected with the situation we have been discussing.

It will surely be agreed that the most individually tragic and nationally disturbing aspects of unemployment is juvenile unemployment. There are about 25,000 wholly unemployed boys and girls in the Special Areas of England and Wales. This represents about two-fifths of the total number of unemployed juveniles in the country, although the population of the Special Areas is only a thirteenth of the population of England and Wales. A similar situation prevails in the vitally important age-group of young men from 18 to 21.

" Many of these young persons," writes the Commissioner for Special Areas in his second Annual Report, " have done practically no work ; they have been brought up in a home where the father has been continuously out of work, and they have little or no conception that a man's ordinary occupation should be such as will provide the means of subsistence for himself and for his family. They have seen their own families and their friends kept for years by the State, and they have come to accept this as a normal condition of life. It is hardly surprising in the circumstances that young persons with this background and upbringing should be ready victims of all manner of demoralizing influences. In short, these young men present in my view the most tragic aspect of the problem of the Special Areas and one fraught with great danger to the State."

We dealt with the question of the " Hard Core " in an earlier chapter, noting the importance of the duration of unemployment. A recent analysis showed that over half the men unemployed in the Special Areas had been out of work for more than a year. And this gives no indication of the number of men who have had but little work for the last five or ten or even fifteen years, during which in many cases depression has persisted.

Finally, it should be emphasized that least of all in the depressed areas is it possible to suggest that unemployment is the fault of the individual. In a pamphlet printed in 1903, under the title of *The Poverty Line*, Mr. Seeholm Rowntree pointed out that " if the men and women in this class (of unemployed) possessed, as a whole, extraordinary energy and perseverance, they might perhaps, notwithstanding physical problems, and a depressing environment, raise themselves to a higher level ; but it is idle to expect from them as a class, virtues and powers far in excess of those characterizing any other section of the community."

However great the energy and perseverance of the unemployed men and women in the depressed areas, they cannot solve their problem of employment. They can, and they very often do, do something to help themselves in the various ways made possible by social service—to which we shall come later on. Some of them work far harder at voluntary activities and local government than they would have to at ordinary employment. I know few busier men than Mr. Stanley Nicholl, of Workington. Mr. J. C. C. Davidson, who conducted the original official investigation into the conditions in West Cumberland, recorded that " the West Cumbrian has preserved the staunch character, good physique and independence which have enabled him to retain in a high degree the virtues of good citizenship and a sense of responsibility. Local Government is carried on in the distressed and partially derelict areas, in many cases by the unemployed themselves, with just the same standards of economy and prudence as one would expect in a prosperous area." Sir Wyndham Portal, now Lord Portal, noted in South Wales that the unemployed members of the County Councils and Urban District

Councils " spoke on their subjects without any reference to the permanent officials, which is quite unlike my experience in the Southern Counties of England." But even these men who so bravely retain the virtues of good citizenship and pass that greatest of all tests of character, the test of adversity, with flying colours, cannot find work to support themselves and their families.

Thus the bare figures themselves, the total of 300,000, the unemployment proportion of 30 per cent., give little idea of the underlying facts. There can be no doubt that in the depressed areas as a whole, particularly if we include the unscheduled but none the less severely hit districts, is concentrated a great deal, probably indeed the major part, of the tragedy, wastage and danger of unemployment.

It was not until 1934 that the National Government awoke to the serious nature of the problem. As the result of considerable public discussion and popular agitation some independent men of standing were appointed to study and report on the position. As we have seen, Mr. Davidson took West Cumberland and Sir Wyndham Portal South Wales ; while the North-East Coast was investigated by Captain Euan Wallace and the Scottish area by Sir Arthur Rose.

These eminent men recorded in detail the facts I have endeavoured thus briefly to outline, they made a thorough examination of the economic possibilities of the areas and they made a number of recommendations.

One of the most outstanding features of their separate reports was the unanimity with which they reached the conclusion that no foreseeable revival of the old industries, on which the prosperity of the areas and the concentration of their population had been based, could absorb more than a limited proportion of the unemployed.   Sir Wyndham Portal made a particularly striking calculation for South Wales.   He assumed a revival of trade sufficient to enable industry in the area to work at full capacity, and included in his calculation the probable effect of such a revival on employment in the minor industries (e.g., building, works of construction and distribution trades).   This, he estimated, would only absorb about half the 80,000 unemployed in the area.

The old industries could not solve the problem. Moreover, as they consisted of the heavy staple industries upon whose recovery the attention of statesmen and economists had been concentrated ever since the War, the Reports could suggest nothing very novel to assist their revival.   Action on new lines was essential.   The most important recommendations in the Reports fall under a few main heads.

The most obvious way to deal with unemployed people surplus to an area is to transfer them somewhere else.   All the Reports stressed the importance of properly organized transfer, particularly of juvenile labour and the younger people generally.   Mr. Davidson stated that a clear and authoritative pronouncement that there will not be work for all in West Cumberland is essential, in order to encourage transfer.   But at the same time he and the other investigators admitted the extreme difficulties inherent in the attachment of the people to their homes.   When transferred they often walk home again.

Another remedy universally stressed was settlement

H

on the land.   All the various forms of such settlement —afforestation schemes, small holdings affording an independent livelihood, " group holdings " or plots up to a quarter or half an acre of land per man cultivated by men working in groups of about 20 and affording partial subsistence, and ordinary allotment cultivation —were considered and strong recommendations made that they should be further explored and pushed forward.

The treatment of public works in the Reports was not quite uniform.   Captain Euan Wallace was the only investigator who showed some measure of disagreement with the very conservative policy of the National Government in this respect.   He recommended that the various schemes put forward in Durham, which, apart from their possible value to the community, were designed to give additional employment, should be reconsidered by the Departments affected in the light of the general conditions prevailing in the area.   In particular, he suggested clearance of some of the derelict factory sites on Tyneside in order to improve the appearance and amenities of the district, work which, as he said, was eminently suitable for unskilled labour, as well as extensive housing schemes.

The other investigators were more cautious and confined their suggestions to works of a more obviously remunerative nature.   Mr. Davidson definitely set his face against " relief schemes as palliatives, and as was to be expected from men of the character of the West Cumbrians, I found that my attitude received the general support."

All the Reports mentioned with approval the efforts made through various forms of Social Service to render the lot of those affected by unemployment tolerable, and recommended that they should be encouraged and supported.

Perhaps the most whole-hearted agreement, however, concerned the establishment of new industries in the Areas. Every investigator urged that every possible effort should be made to encourage and attract new industries and recommended the establishment of some sort of Development Council to this end where one did not exist. But none was particularly optimistic about the possible results. Mr. Davidson noted that the Manchester University investigators who had preceded him had examined a large number of suggestions for new industries, of which only four appeared to merit examination, and in no case did subsequent enquiry lead to the conclusion that the immediate employment of substantial numbers of work-people was likely. Captain Euan Wallace remarked somewhat regretfully that the State was not in a position to direct the location of any new British industry, or even to offer inducements towards a particular area. Sir Wyndham Portal, who considered the question most carefully, definitely suggested the offering of such inducements in the shape of Government contracts and actual subsidies, as well as the placing of a Government factory in South Wales. He also remarked that the already existing Industrial Development Council of South Wales was an energetic body, but without any real power, as no big industrialists took an active part on the Council. Sir Arthur Rose stated firmly that the direction of industry in the sense of coercion by the Government as to the place where new industries may be started was definitely unsound, but he believed the Government could do something to help, for example, by directing more Government orders to the Clyde. The investigators were obviously hampered in their consideration of this problem by the fact that they had practically no successful experiments in the influencing of industrial location to work on.

After receiving their Reports, the Government recognized that the case for special treatment had been established. The " Special Areas " were definitely scheduled ; £2,000,000 was voted for a Special Areas Fund ; and two Commissions were appointed, one for England and Wales and one for Scotland. They have been engaged on their task since the autumn of 1934.

The second Report of Mr. Malcolm Stewart, the Commissioner for England and Wales, was issued in February, 1936. It gives full details of everything that has been done for the Special Areas under the powers of the Commissioner and in co-operation with him. Let us examine it under the five main heads of the investigators' recommendations—transfer, land settlement, public works, social services, and new industries.

During the year from December, 1934, to November, 1935, 21,620 people were transferred out of the Special Areas of England and Wales including those transferred for land settlement. Nearly 6,600 of those were boys and girls under 18. This was done under the various Ministry of Labour schemes, but it was, of course, assisted by the Commissioner and by organizations subsidized by him.

In the matter of land settlement, a number of schemes were promoted through the Land Settlement Association. The principal method chosen was to purchase an agricultural estate and to settle groups of about 40 families on it with the supervision and assistance of a resident Warden.   Houses are built, and each family receives a market-garden holding of about five acres and the necessary stock—40 pigs and 150–200 head of poultry is about the average.   It is too early to say how successful this settlement will be, but the Commissioner states that a programme has been approved which should enable about 2,000 families to be established in small holdings by the summer of 1937.

As distinct from this full-time settlement where the men are expected to become completely independent, " Group holding " and allotment movements have been encouraged within the Special Areas themselves.   A " group holding " is really a large allotment of a quarter to half an acre and serves as a training-ground for would-be settlers as well as providing occupation and a slightly improved standard of living for men too old to settle.   About 1,500 men were being helped in this way at the date of the Report, and a further 1,600 had been given allotments.

A scheme of afforestation in or near the Special Areas was proposed, to enable 1,000 families to be ultimately settled as forest holders, but it had not yet been put into practice.

In spite of the rather doubtful attitude expressed in the reports of the investigators, the Commissioner seems to have been most active in assisting public works of various kinds.   Grants were approved towards over 150 separate schemes undertaken by local authorities, whose total estimated cost was nearly £1,900,000.   A Housing Association was also set up in the North-

Eastern Area, to which the Commissioner is prepared to make grants.

Probably the most effective action taken by the Commissioner has been in stimulating and supporting social service. He makes a large block grant to assist the National Council of Social Service in its work of organizing social clubs and group activities among the unemployed ; he finances the very successful " amenity schemes," under which a group of unemployed men are provided with a midday meal and the necessary materials, tools and working kit to make playing-fields, tennis courts, bowling greens and similar amenities for the use of their community ; he gives grants (generally through the National Council of Social Service) to the various voluntary bodies working among young people—like the Y.M.C.A., Boy Scouts and Girl Guides and so on ; he helps district nursing and health services generally ; he finances holiday camps and permanent Social Settlements. There can be no question—and I am speaking with some measure of personal experience—that he has done a great deal towards making life tolerable in spite of the tragedy of unemployment—above all by helping people to help themselves.

But what of industry ; above all, what of the establishment of new industries upon which the investigators laid such stress ? Here the Commissioner had to record almost complete failure.

He had, it is true, helped to set up and finance Industrial Development Councils in the North-East Area and in West Cumberland—no mean task incidentally in view of local prejudice and bickering —and he had made a grant towards the already existing

South Wales Council. He had also set in motion schemes for industrial Trading Estates on the Slough model. But the only new industrial development of note within the whole of the Special Areas was the decision of Richard Thomas and Company to take over, reconstruct and re-open Ebbw Vale Steelworks—a development, be it noted, in the old heavy industry. Not one single case of the establishment or progress of a new light industry does the Commissioner find worth while recording. And a promising scheme for a new steelworks at Jarrow, which he mentions as likely to go through, has since been practically vetoed by the highly cartellised iron and steel industry under rather dubious circumstances.

Such was the measure of achievement the Commissioner was able to point to after over a year's work. It is perhaps not surprising that in spite of the transference of over 20,000 people, in spite of a very considerable measure of revival in precisely those heavy industries upon which the Special Areas depend, the number of registered unemployed only dropped by 26,000 during the year from about 344,000 to about 318,000. Unless wholesale depopulation over a period of twenty years or so be regarded as a solution, there can surely be no doubt that the key to the puzzle of the Special Areas has not yet been found.

Nothing could be more unfair than to blame Mr. Malcolm Stewart, his District Commissioners, and his staff of able civil servants for this meagre result. What are the real reasons ?

Mr. Malcolm Stewart begins his first Report, published in July, 1935, with a number of quotations from statements made by members of the Government during the passage of the Act governing his powers, the Special Areas (Development and Improvement) Act. They are deserving of study in full, but I must content myself with giving some extracts.

The Chancellor of the Exchequer, Mr. Neville Chamberlain, said that what was wanted was " something more rapid, more direct, less orthodox, if you like, than the ordinary plan." The Government had " resolved to cut through all the ordinary methods and adopt a plan . . . more suitable to these special conditions than the methods which, in the ordinary course, could be applied to such a problem." The Commissioners were going to " be given a very wide discretion. They must not be afraid of trying experiments even if those experiments fail."

The Parliamentary Secretary to the Ministry of Labour, Mr. R. S. Hudson, spoke of the difficulty of putting into practice valuable ideas " if you go through the elaborate procedure of Government Departments to make sure that every single thing you do will stand the criticism of the Public Accounts Committee of this House and questions across the floor." The Government believed that it was " possible to cut that procedure short and to go behind a great deal of red tape." The Commissioners had been set up " precisely to enable experiments on a very large scale of every sort and kind to be made in the depressed areas." And the Paymaster-General, Lord Rochester, reinforced this by saying : " The first striking point, therefore, in the proposals in the Bill, is that the Commissioners have wide powers which they can freely exercise."

To meet the general criticism that the sum of

£2,000,000 was too small, several members of the Government, including the Prime Minister, insisted that it was merely a sort of token vote to give the Commissioners a start. Lord Rochester even referred to it as " merely a preliminary figure for the three months ending next March." The Minister of Labour, Mr. Oliver Stanley, said that the Commissioners would " start off with enough money to make it quite certain that they will be enabled to undertake any experiment and work which they think is necessary." Thereafter they would, of course, have more money " as and when the Government and Parliament think that more money should be given to them."

In the light of these statements it might reasonably have been assumed that the Commissioners had been given a job of work and told to get on with it, subject only to the general approval of the Government, much as Sir John Reith gets on with the work of the B.B.C. This, however, was by no means the case.

Mr. Stewart pointed out that in fact he had to seek the sanction of the Minister of Labour to all main lines of policy. " The Minister of Labour is responsible to Parliament for the way in which the money voted is expended, and the Permanent Secretary of the Ministry of Labour as Accounting Officer will have to answer for the Commissioner to the Public Accounts Committee. These limitations are no doubt necessary in order to conform to Parliamentary practice in regard to finance, but they clearly *make the Commissioner as much subject to orthodox financial control as any Government Department* (my italics). Whilst they may not actually hamper the freedom and initiative of the Commissioner so far as making proposals is concerned, they do result in restricting his powers to carry these proposals into effect."

Somehow the red tape which Mr. Hudson proposed to go behind seems difficult to evade. But another limitation of the Commissioner's powers is even more serious.

Except in the matter of small holdings, he is not allowed to supplement a specific grant made or offered by a Government Department, or to offer a grant to a local authority for any service for which a specific grant is payable by any Government Department. For example, if the Minister of Transport offers a local authority a grant towards making a new road and the local authority, as is not unusual in the Special Areas, cannot afford to pay the balance, the Commissioner cannot help. Nor can he help local authorities to construct roads, bridges, tunnels, canals or quays, or to develop any education service, since Government Departments are able, though they may very well not be willing, to do so.

Mr. Stewart points out that one serious effect of this embargo is to prevent him from giving any grant towards the cost of the roadways which are an essential and integral part of schemes of site improvement for industrial development. Though in theory such roads are eligible for a grant from the Road Fund, in fact they have no through traffic value and will never receive such a grant.

It may be asked why the Ministry of Transport cannot make exceptions to help the special problem of the Special Areas. Mr. Stewart admits that it is within his powers to ask them to do so. But they are bound by their precedents and " general standards " (words which Mr. Stewart has surely heard many more times in the last two years than in the whole of the rest of his life) and he appreciates the difficulty which the Departments find " in departing from their general standards in specific cases—a difficulty which would have been met if the Commissioner had been given power to make grants out of the Special Areas Fund, the object of which was to meet the special needs of the areas."

This difficulty was due to a legal interpretation of the word " payable." The lawyers have also insisted that the Act does not allow the Commissioner to do or assist anything outside Great Britain. He can thus neither promote emigration nor even help the Development Councils to advertise their areas abroad. Yet another legal opinion has prevented the provision of hostels for people transferred from the Special Areas because hostels do not of themselves " afford employment or occupation."

The strict limitation of the Commissioners' powers and the scheduled Areas has also been detrimental, particularly in South Wales, where Cardiff, Newport and Swansea have been excluded from what is " in essence one economic unit."

Above all, the Commissioner can give no financial assistance towards the establishment or development of new industries, or for that matter of any industries, operating for profit. Mr. Stewart recognizes this limitation of his powers as " clearly desirable, though it debars the giving of any help in a direction where help is badly needed." But in the long run, assuming the retention of our present economic system, only " industries operating for profit " can save the Special

Areas. This is a subject I shall deal with at greater length later on.

In the light of the Commissioner's explanation of his powers, it is surely no exaggeration to describe the " very wide discretion " as a snare and a delusion. One cannot help wondering whether Mr. Stewart read his Act, or at any rate had it authoritatively interpreted to him, before he accepted his purely honorary but none the less onerous job.

The legal limitations, however, are by no means the whole story. The great difficulties which he has to face in persuading authorities and organizations to spend money where he himself is unable to offer financial help can readily be imagined. What is perhaps not so easy to realize is the difficulty of securing effective action even when monetary inducements can be given.

The Commissioner has almost invariably adopted the method of working indirectly, through the existing machinery of Government and other bodies. He probably had no choice. He could not set up a really extensive organization himself—incidentally he cannot appoint a single member of his staff without the consent of both the Ministry of Labour and of the Treasury. But, above all, to work through existing bodies by giving them " grant-aid " and otherwise is the traditional British way of government.

I doubt whether it would be possible to find any better example of the limitations of democratic procedure in general than the experience of the Commissioner himself, his local Commissioners in the various districts, and his staff. Instead of getting down to the job and doing it, their lives must have been one long consideration of the question who—what individual, organization, or public body—was competent for what, and how best to persuade them to act. Indeed in many cases even this resource of persuasion was denied to them. More particularly whenever anything voluntary was in question, for example the " amenity " or other social service schemes whose importance we have stressed, the Commissioner and his representatives have been obliged to sit back and wait for the initiative to come from the voluntary bodies. Even with government and local government organizations they have often had to walk very warily for fear of treading on prominent and touchy toes.

Then there was the problem of divided competence —nearly every major scheme was dependent on the assent of various authorities not all of whom may have been good bed-fellows. It is not difficult to imagine the endless conferences, committees and dissensions, the checks and obstacles and jealousies. And all the while the unemployed men and women in the Special Areas stood at the street-corners.

But whatever difficulties the Commissioner may have had to contend with in dealing with governmental and voluntary bodies, they were nothing to the obstacles he met in handling " industries operating for profit."

In his first Report Mr. Stewart showed that he clearly recognized the vital importance of this question of productive industry with a remarkable passage which really sums up the whole problem of the Special Areas.

" The Special Areas," he wrote, " are in their present unfortunate position owing to the decline of the main industries, coal-mining, shipbuilding and iron and steel, which attracted such large numbers of workers to them during the nineteenth century under more prosperous conditions. It seems unlikely that these industries will again employ the numbers engaged in them even up to ten years ago. During the period of prosperity large communities with full equipment of railways, roads, houses, schools and other municipal and social services were created. Many millions of pounds were spent in building up these services. A large proportion of the inhabitants have been associated with the Areas for several generations ; they are bound to the Areas by ties of home and family and religion, by local patriotism and, especially in Wales, by a fervent national spirit and, sometimes, a distinctive language. It is natural, therefore, that wherever one goes in the Areas one should be met by the demand that something should be done to attract fresh industries. . . . This is the general request, and I regard it as at once the most important and the most difficult of my duties to try to satisfy it."

In pursuance of this aim the Commissioner sent out in co-operation with the Federation of British Industries a short questionnaire to industrial firms outside the Special Areas. He inserted at the same time in the journal of each trade a short article explaining his objects, which were broadly speaking to find out the general attitude of industry to enterprise in the Special Areas. A few simple questions were asked ; for example, whether the firm had considered a site in the Special Areas during the past five years and, if so, why the suggestion had been turned down, and whether the firm was prepared to consider the matter again. As the Commissioner pointed out, the completion and return of the questionnaire entailed no expense and involved the minimum of labour.

In the first place only half the industrial associations affiliated to the F.B.I. were prepared to co-operate to the extent of supplying addresses. Of the 5,829 firms whose addresses were procured, 4,066 firms did not bother to reply, while 1,313 firms gave unqualified negative replies to all questions. Of the 450 remaining more helpful replies 386 gave qualified negatives to all questions and only 64 answered a question in the affirmative. Thirty-eight firms said that they had established new works or branches in the Special Areas during the past few years ; 35 said they had considered a site and decided against it, while only 12 said that they were prepared to consider the matter. No wonder that the Commissioner wrote of the " lack of interest in the Special Areas shown by industry in general."

We have by now gained some idea of the tragedy of the Special Areas. It will be remembered that we were seeking the right subject for bold economic experiment, a subject which would command the greatest possible measure of agreement. Is it too much to suggest that we have found it ?

But the experiment must be bold and far-reaching. The major tragedy of the Special Areas has its counterpart in what may without exaggeration be described as the minor tragedy of the frustration of the able and devoted men who were appointed to tackle the problem. It was not their fault that their efforts have fallen " like snow upon the desert's dusty face." The Special Areas Act is about to come up for renewal ; will the lessons of the Commissioner's experience upon which we have briefly touched be fully borne in mind in renewing it ?

Finally we have begun to realize that the outstanding

question in the Special Areas is that of the stimulation of productive industry " for purposes of gain." No amount of " natural " revival of the old industries will suffice ; for it is already occurring and barely touches the fringe of the problem.

Here the failure has been most complete. But here the Commissioner leaves us a ray of hope which will be the guiding light of the next chapters. The arguments advanced by the few firms who took the trouble to reply helpfully to his questionnaire showed " no single well-defined and insurmountable obstacle standing in the way (of enterprise in the Areas), but rather a variety of vaguely defined and probably vaguely felt prejudices which may be overcome if the right means to combat them can be discovered."

CHAPTER VI

Not long ago I was asked by a friend, a leading international hosiery manufacturer, to advise and assist
him in the establishment of a branch factory in England.
He was taking a short holiday over here at the time, and
I proposed that he should accompany me on a trip to
see for himself the industrial possibilities involved.

Before setting out, my friend suggested that we
might enquire about the situation in the suburbs of
London. After all, London was the principal distributing centre in the country, the key to the vast and
prosperous market of the South. What about a
factory, say, on Western Avenue ?

A few minutes at the Ministry of Labour disposed of
this idea. Before a manufacturer can sell his goods he
has to make them. The basis of all manufacture is
good and steady labour. Not only was there no
possibility of obtaining round London any workers
skilled in the particular direction required, but it would
have been exceedingly difficult to get sufficient adaptable and satisfactory men and girls to train.

So we turned our backs on London and proceeded to
the Mecca of the hosiery trade, which as everybody
knows is Leicester. Practically every English connection of my friend's, particularly those in the trade,

had told him that Leicester and its district was the place, indeed the only place, for his factory. But there we were met by the same difficulty. If my friend wanted labour in any quantity he would have to import it, and as for getting skilled hosiery workers, except by the dubious method of bribing them to desert their existing employment, it was quite out of the question. Moreover, that was a game that two could play, and when he had imported and trained his labour, there was a pretty good chance of its being tempted away by other factories with the offer of higher wages. We heard, indeed, of a German hosiery concern which after starting up in Leicester had been obliged to abandon production on these grounds. Finally, factory sites were expensive and there were no suitable factories to be sold or let.

At the beginning of our trip I had suggested that we might find in one of the depressed areas what we were seeking, so that we were not excessively disappointed. After a few more brief and fruitless enquiries in the prosperous Midlands, we went on to two depressed districts, one scheduled and the other not.

In both we were welcomed by a courteous and helpful Development Council which provided full information regarding factory sites, vacant factories, available labour, transport and every other need of the industrialist ; we were taken to view the most suitable sites ; we were informed that any concern starting business could be certain of the full co-operation of all the authorities, local government bodies and so on ; in one case we even learnt that the Further Education Committee was prepared at its own expense to purchase a machine of the type my friend employed and use it to train, free of all charge, young workers for the new factory. Needless to say, ample labour was available, and informal talks with the local inhabitants near the suggested sites left no doubt in my mind that any firm starting up and treating its workers decently could be certain of building up a really loyal and permanently attached staff—the dream of every intelligent industrialist.

My friend has at the time of writing not yet made his choice, and in the circumstances the districts in question had better be nameless. But the moral is surely plain.

All over the prosperous districts the difficulty of obtaining good labour is rapidly increasing. Firms considering expansion are obliged to postpone it ; men who are building up businesses from small beginnings find themselves seriously hampered ; sometimes even people who wish to start production are unable to do so. These difficulties are reinforced by the high price of suitable factory sites and the lack of vacant factories —many business men who wish to try out production do not want to go to the expense of building. Whether these developments have already reached the stage of being a serious deterrent to enterprise is a moot point, but they will undoubtedly become so.

In the depressed areas, scheduled and unscheduled, the picture is entirely reversed. Sites are cheap ; factories can be bought or rented for the proverbial song ; and above all ample and excellent labour is available.

It is sometimes objected that the labour in the depressed areas is difficult to handle, that the Trade Unions have a bad reputation and that extreme forms of Socialism and Communism are rife. In view of the situation we have been discussing it would hardly be surprising if it were so.

In point of fact, except perhaps in South Wales, it is extraordinary how little ground the extremists have won. I have rarely seen a more pathetic and bedraggled little meeting than one addressed by Mr. Wal Hannington at Cleator Moor—perhaps the most derelict town in West Cumberland ; the Communists in a London or a Birmingham suburb could do incomparably better. As Mr. G. D. H. Cole once pointed out to me in criticism of Marx, prosperous workers often fall the most ready converts to Socialist doctrines; and while labour troubles have hitherto been infrequent in the prosperous South and Midlands, there are distinct signs that the workers there are becoming increasingly conscious of their strength and bargaining power.

The labour troubles in the depressed areas took place for the most part in the heyday of their prosperity. The Trade Unions have had a hard lesson. There can be no doubt that they would welcome new industries with open arms ; no one could have been more helpful or more enthusiastically receptive of the ideas I am endeavouring to put forward in this book than the local Trade Union officials. Incidentally this attitude was noted by the investigators of the Special Areas, and Captain Euan Wallace pointed out that in Northumberland and Durham the average number of working days lost by disputes per person involved was $2 \cdot 2$, $3 \cdot 1$ and $13 \cdot 0$ for the years 1930, 1931 and 1932 respectively, as against $14 \cdot 0$, $14 \cdot 2$ and $17 \cdot 1$ for Great Britain as a whole.

Another point often raised regarding the labour in the depressed areas is the question of skill. Most of the older unemployed are, of course, skilled men in their particular trades of coal-mining, iron and steel, and so on. But naturally comparatively few are skilled in the new light industries which it is so desirable to attract.

But it is an outstanding feature of these new light industries that for the most part they call rather for semi-skilled machine-minders than for highly-skilled technicians. Miners in particular, who constitute such a large proportion of the unemployed in the areas, are remarkably adaptable all-round men, and in this connection it is perhaps not irrelevant that in some parts of Germany miners have been accustomed to doing textile work in the summer and mining in the winter. The essential thing is that men should have a " feel " in their fingers and be accustomed to the methods of industry, conditions which are much more readily found in a population which has been employed in industry than among workers drawn, say, from agriculture. Moreover it would be by no means true to say that no skill in the light industries is available in the areas ; there have been some light industries there in the past, and, for example, an industrialist of my acquaintance who needs cabinet-makers is going to Tyneside where cabinet-making has been an important subsidiary aspect of shipbuilding. In the depressed parts of Lancashire, of course, an adaptable textile skill is available which must be unequalled in the world. Finally, we have already noted the willingness of the Further Education Authorities to assist in training workers for specific purposes. There can be no question that skilled workers are easier to obtain in the depressed areas than in the vast majority of the prosperous districts.

The two remaining stock objections to enterprise in the areas are high rates and remoteness from markets.

The first thing to note is that rates are by no means invariably high—in West Cumberland, for example, they are lower than in many thoroughly prosperous districts. But even where they are high, notably in parts of South Wales, the derating of industrial premises greatly reduces the burden of industry. Moreover, in view of the extreme anxiety in the areas to attract new industries, it should generally be easy for anybody proposing to start up to negotiate an assessment with the Rating Authorities which makes the enterprise possible.

On the question of remoteness from markets I am not at all sure, as far as the Northern areas are concerned, that the real balance of advantage is not the other way.

In marketing goods it is not so much the absolute consuming capacity of a population which counts but the possibility of exploiting it. All over the prosperous South and Midlands high-pressure salesmen have for years been exercising their concentrated wiles. Every distributor, every shop, has been visited over and over again ; every marketing possibility has been seized upon and worked out to the limit by keen and active brains. To get into markets which have thus been gone over with the small-toothed comb beloved of detective-story writers, again and again, is becoming increasingly difficult.

Moreover there are distinct signs in the South of the rate of expansion slowing up, partly, it may be, for the reasons already suggested. Building—always a good barometer of activity—seems to be slacking off. If the

South really is reaching saturation-point this cannot fail to have a serious effect on marketing possibilities.

The best markets and by far the easiest markets to get into are expanding markets.   Hitherto this feature has constituted the main attraction of the South.   But to-day it is in the North that recovery is now most evident and expansion is taking place most rapidly ; it is chiefly in the North that the millions to be spent on rearmament will be translated into a demand for radios, motor-cars, bicycles, gramophones, refrigerators, silk stockings and all the hundred and one products of the new light industries.   As Mr. St. Clare Grondona, the District Commissioner for the most isolated of the Special Areas, West Cumberland, has pointed out, there are 13 million potential customers living within 100 miles of Whitehaven.

The older industrial districts, with the tragic exceptions we are discussing, are coming into their own again.   But it is surely possible that those exceptions will not remain exceptions.   Once activity in the depressed and Special Areas gets going, as soon as the doles become wages on an appreciable scale, there will be a very rapid expansion of purchasing power with corresponding marketing possibilities.

It is thus by no means unlikely that in the next few years industries in the depressed Northern areas will prove to be in a better strategic position than those in the South, that it will be more satisfactory to distribute, say, from Leeds than from London.   Moreover, in any case, transport is not a large item in the cost-sheets of most light industries.

Indeed it is extraordinarily difficult to say what are the chief factors influencing the location of the light and secondary industries which are playing so large a part to-day.   In some cases, of course, the original reasons have perhaps been lost sight of but the tradition goes on. Northampton is the place for boots, Leicester for hosiery, Bradford for woollens.   Auxiliary industries have developed to assist the main industry and they, of course, are lacking elsewhere.   None the less there are many outstanding examples of successful enterprises starting in comparative isolation.   In the boot and shoe trade, to take only one instance, there have been Clark, of Street in Somerset, Somervell's K-boot factory in Kendal, Sir H. Trickett's initiation of the slipper trade at Waterfoot in Lancashire, while the spectacular Bata enterprise makes a point, in every country, of being entirely on its own.

In the new industries tradition has, of course, played no part.   Nor have any other obvious reasons been operative ;   they use electric power and have not needed to be near coal or iron ore, or in a damp climate like the Lancashire cotton mills.   Perhaps they started in the South because in the immediate post-War period labour was easier to come by and easier to handle there, perhaps because the development of munition factories during the War had showed that industry could be successfully operated where nobody had thought of industry before.   Perhaps—and this is an important point to which we shall refer again—because industrialists preferred living there.

However that may be, there are strong grounds for believing that many of the innumerable new and imposing factories which crowd such places as the Great West Road and Western Avenue have been put there because the district was fashionable, just as men elect to live in " W.1," or on an attractive housing estate round a golf course. They might just as well have been set up in the older industrial areas where they are so badly needed. And to-day, unless the whole basis of our argument is unsound, those older areas, notably the depressed and Special Areas, seem to offer the soundest prospects from a purely commercial point of view. The depressed areas are the areas of real opportunity.

It may perhaps be objected that if this were the case business men would have realized it and acted accordingly. The theory of free enterprise is based on the idea that business, like water, always finds its own level of maximum profit-earning capacity and of maximum service to the community. To-day the second proposition is widely disputed, but few opponents of the existing system will be found to dispute the first.

In fact, however, the simile of some sticky liquid like treacle would be much more apt. There is often a great time-lag between the appearance of economic opportunities and their utilization, while undoubtedly many opportunities are never seized at all. The great fortunes of business are generally made by men who hit upon or take up some simple idea for which the time is ripe and who have the energy to put it into practice. Posterity, hearing the story, often wonders how on earth the great man's contemporaries and predecessors could have been so dense. Yet had the man not appeared, the idea would have lain dormant until the occasion for putting it into practice was past.

The importance of leadership in industry can never be sufficiently emphasized. The

economic life of a community is not an impersonal
mechanical structure but a living entity dependent
above all upon the efforts and energies of individual
men and women. Even our modern highly-organized
and integrated companies and concerns and trusts will
generally be found to have been created and to be
inspired by the leadership of one or two dominating
personalities—Lord Ashfield and Mr. Pick of the
London Passenger Transport Board are outstanding
instances in a semi-socialized enterprise. Soviet Russia
is rapidly learning this lesson, however opposed to
classic Marxian doctrine it may be ; the famous
Stakhanovist movement is merely a method of
encouraging leadership and initiative to rise out of the
ranks.

In fact, industry—and, above all, new industries
and new developments in industry—depends on
industrialists. Under the existing economic system
and, for that matter, if the example of Russia is to be
trusted, under any economic system, the recovery of
the depressed areas can only be secured by stimulating
enterprise and initiative among the population of the
areas or importing it from outside.

Only the other day a well-known industrialist stayed
with me for a holiday week-end in West Cumberland.
He looked at the obviously fertile soil and thought of
canning factories ; he saw the United Steel Company's
plant at Workington (which produces a grade of steel
very suitable for cans) and wondered why no secondary
industries had developed to work up the steel produced ; he saw the little Herdwick sheep with their
short, hard, durable wool and thought of a domestic
industry round a central organization to produce

bathing suits and pullovers; he asked whether a domestic wooden toy industry on similar lines had been considered (there is the basis for one in Cleator Moor); and he was astonished that nobody had established shoe factories to work up the excellent leather produced by the Whitehaven and Maryport tanneries.

Most of these ideas were not original; some may be impracticable. But they were the immediate and wholly spontaneous reactions of an energetic and active-minded man to a district which many people give up as hopeless. The stimulus which such men exercise wherever they may be can scarcely be overestimated, and the fact that so many of them have departed elsewhere constitutes one of the major difficulties of the depressed areas. As the Commissioner wrote in his first Report, the whole experience of the past shows that prosperity can only be brought about by " the enterprise, the foresight and courage of individuals."

We are now at last in a position to see the basic problem of the depressed areas. It boils down to this : how can industrialists be persuaded to take action which, so far as human foresight can tell, would be economically sound and profitable, how can they be induced to establish industries in the areas instead of in the over-developed South and Midlands ?

Left to themselves, industrialists may in the long run be forced in the desired direction by the steady pressure of the labour shortage and the other influences we have been considering. But these influences work slowly, almost imperceptibly. They may merely have the effect of hampering enterprise in the prosperous districts without stimulating it elsewhere. Economic opportunities are elusive ; once missed they may not recur, and the wealth and prosperity which might have been created is lost for good.   The last slump occurred long before the capital and labour in the depressed areas had been fully set working ; the next slump may again catch industrialists before they have realized that a great chance is presenting itself.

Industrialists are the most conservative of business men.   Their conservatism is not the result of an extra dose of original sin ; it is due to the nature of their occupation.   It is not difficult for merchants or bankers to move their place of business ; it is an extremely simple matter for them to set up a branch wherever they like.   Their assets are often wholly intangible ; at the most they consist of a comparatively easily movable stock of goods.   The stock-in-trade of an industrialist is far more complicated.   He needs large and specially designed buildings, heavy machinery, a considerable number of skilled workers.   He has to plan well in advance and cannot easily adapt himself to changed circumstances.   His business is extremely difficult to establish and it may take years before he begins to earn a return for the capital he puts in.   Thus it is scarcely surprising that once industrialists are well established and producing a profitable line it should be difficult to move them or even to induce them to embark on new enterprise away from their main factories.

To these economic factors, moreover, must be added the personal factor—we must never forget that we are dealing with individuals.   The prosperous leaders of the new industries are getting along quite well in the South.   It is only natural that they should like their comfortable lives in Surrey or Herts, their golf at

Sunningdale or Addington or Moor Park. Suppose that the question of the establishment of a new branch factory in a depressed area is about to come up at a board meeting, and that the night before the senior executive who would have to go mentions the matter to his wife, who protests that there will be nothing to do and nobody to know, not even a decent hairdresser ! Is he not likely, most probably with a perfectly clear conscience and perhaps without even realizing that he has been influenced, to go to his meeting the next morning and talk of labour troubles and Communism, of the remoteness from markets, of high rates, with the result that the proposal is turned down ?

The reluctance of business men, even of merchants, to make a move or to adapt themselves to changing circumstances has perhaps never been better demonstrated than by the sad story of the merchants and industrialists of Bruges. In the Middle Ages Bruges was a thriving port. The sea-going ships of those times came right up to the town, which was the chief centre of the famous woollen trade and manufacture of Flanders. Gradually the channels began to silt up and the ships to grow larger. They could no longer get to Bruges. The rival merchants of Antwerp and Rotterdam had better harbours and made use of them ; trade as well as manufacture started to shift. But nothing could shift the merchants and manufacturers of Bruges. Instead of moving where opportunity was waiting they sat, generation after generation, in their tall houses on the canal banks and watched their great wealth dwindle to nothing.

Yet history also shows the possibility of transplanting enterprise, or rather enterprising men, on a large scale.

The great British woollen industry was started by much the same Flemish weavers as those who stayed at Bruges ; only the former were goaded into emigrating by persecution while the latter were allowed to stagnate. Persecution was also responsible for the migration of the Huguenots, to whom British trade and industry owes so great a debt.

To persecute industrialists in the prosperous districts seems rather a drastic method of solving the problem of the depressed areas. Yet somehow enterprise must be stimulated, somehow men must be found who will put into the reconstruction of those areas the same energy and initiative as were originally applied to the develop- ment of their natural resources. There is no other way.

Is it possible within a capitalist system to influence economic development in directions which are socially desirable ? I have endeavoured to show in the fore- going chapters that the question lies at the core of our economic and political struggles to-day. Upon the answer which we can give to it the whole future of our industrial civilization may well depend.

I believe that question can be answered in the affirmative. But in any case let us try and see. Here is another sense in which the depressed areas offer a great opportunity. They afford the occasion for a far- reaching and comprehensive experiment in the social direction of economic development. It is an experi- ment which fulfils the condition that it should command the greatest possible measure of public approval—surely few men in this country and none who knows the depressed areas could be found to deny its vital importance. Here the principal objection to " planning," that the planners are not all-wise and are likely to plan wrongly, loses most of its force, at any rate as far as the main object of stimulating industry in the depressed areas is concerned. The goodwill is there, among all classes and even in all districts. How can we make use of it ?

CHAPTER VII

SOME PRACTICAL PROPOSALS

THE word " plan " has been so used and abused that it is best to avoid it here. Moreover the suggestions I am putting forward in this chapter do not constitute a plan at all in the sense of a fully co-ordinated scheme. To produce such a scheme for all the depressed areas is not merely entirely beyond my powers and knowledge ; it seems to me very doubtful whether any satisfactory planned Minerva could spring fully armed from the brain even of a governmental Jove. My aim is rather to suggest a method, a method of practical experiment based on the central idea that only new enterprise " for purposes of gain," indeed only energetic men capable of starting up and carrying through this enterprise, can in the long run save the areas.

The first thing to note is that this stimulation of profit-making or private enterprise by the State is nothing new, even in the most orthodox capitalist countries. It is usually done by the obvious method of providing a direct pecuniary incentive.

Tariffs are universal in the world to-day, and tariffs are merely a way of giving a differential advantage to industry at home. The chief difference between tariffs and direct subsidies, which are also by no means rare, is that in the one case the consumer pays all or most of the cost ; while in the other the money comes out of the pockets of the taxpayer.

Now while tariffs can obviously only be used to a limited extent to help industry in the depressed areas, since the advantage they give is spread over the whole country, there is no such difficulty about subsidies. We give over £33,000,000 annually to agriculture and £2,000,000 to tramp shipping; why should we not subsidize enterprise, or at any rate new enterprise, in the areas where it is so urgently needed ? Why has the National Government put the paralysing limitation on the activities of the Commissioners that they should neither start nor give pecuniary assistance to enterprises for purposes of gain ?

In his first Report, Mr. Malcolm Stewart stated that he agreed with this limitation of his powers. He may have remembered Speenhamland; he may have shrunk from the responsibility of having to face innumerable demands for subsidies to individual private enterprises. But these objections would not apply to regular financial assistance on a clearly-limited basis to all businesses starting up in the areas. To exempt enterprises which are prepared to take the risk of launching out in a depressed area, say, from rates or income-tax for a few years, or even to give a subsidy per man employed as has been done in Germany, would certainly be no more objectionable than to allow a great vested interest to grow up and profit perpetually at the taxpayers' expense as in the case of sugar beet.

The Government are probably afraid of industrialists accusing them of subsidizing competition from the depressed areas. But this argument applies in some degree to all special assistance to the areas. Right

K

from the start, the Government must be prepared to face this accusation. To stimulate competition with existing industries from within the depressed areas is a vital feature of any programme for their rehabilitation. Moreover, only competition from the areas will make the average industrialist notice their advantages. Business men pay attention to successful " enterprises for purposes of gain " and to nothing else. If objections of unfair competition are raised by interested parties the Government can surely put forward the unanswerable argument that enterprise could not be stimulated without inducements and that the interests of the unemployed had to be considered first.

Established policies, however, are difficult to change, and I am not basing the proposals in this chapter on the granting of subsidies to enterprise. I merely wish to make the point that in order to get business men moving some inducements or advantages must be offered in the depressed areas. There must be some readiness to depart from established precedents and practice in favour of the areas. As we have seen, the very existence of the Commissioners is a recognition of the need for this, and unless they, or whoever may be the most appropriate body, are ready to give special treatment to the Special Areas in this vital matter of industrial enterprise the whole paraphernalia is but an empty shell.

It may be objected here that I am knocking at open doors. In response to urgent recommendations by the Commissioners that some way of stimulating private enterprise should be found, the Special Areas Reconstruction Association, generally known as S.A.R.A., has recently been set up with a capital of £1,000,000. The capital is being provided from private sources, but the Government assumes a proportion of the risk involved. Its declared object is to encourage enterprise in the Special Areas by the granting of loans.

S.A.R.A. received the usual Parliamentary send-off and widespread publicity which incidentally led many people into the erroneous belief that the Government was providing £1,000,000 for the Special Areas instead of merely a contingent guarantee against loss. It —or should one say she ?—has only been operating for a few months, so that it is not yet possible to form a definite judgment on the prospects of success. But to judge from the opinions and reports of many who have been in contact with the new organization, there can be little doubt that it suffers from very serious limitations.

First of all, the amount of individual loans is limited to £10,000. This rules out at once assistance to enterprises of any size. Presumably the theory is that such enterprises are in a position to raise money through the usual City channels, by public issue or otherwise. That may be so, but obviously in such a case there is no particular inducement to go into the depressed areas.

Where loans can be granted it is presumably intended that they should act as a special incentive to enterprise. This must surely imply that their terms should be better, whether as regards interest rates or as regards the security demanded, than terms obtainable elsewhere. If S.A.R.A. is merely going to offer much the same facilities as those provided by any bank ; if, for example, it is going to charge four or five per cent. or even more, and to ask for, say, double the amount of the advance as security, it seems hardly worth while setting up an elaborate organization at the public expense.

It may perhaps be objected here that the aim of S.A.R.A. is not to offer an incentive to industrialists to go into the Special Areas, but to give additional help to small enterprises established there, where the banks may be especially cautious owing to bitter past experience. This view seems to be held in some responsible quarters. But it certainly implies a serious limitation, particularly in view of the lack of initiative within the Areas noted by the Commissioner. Is there any reason to suppose that there are large numbers of established business men in districts thoroughly soaked in the atmosphere of depression who will be induced to launch out on borrowed money by the offer of terms little better than those usually obtainable ?

The Prime Minister, at the time of the formation of S.A.R.A., made use of a significant phrase. The function of the new organization, he said, should be to " back the man." His meaning is obvious. Instead of considering mainly the formal security offered, as the present large-scale banking organizations are bound to do, S.A.R.A. should grant loans as far as possible on the basis of its estimate of the initiative and ability of individual men.

The idea is not new. It was discussed at length by the Macmillan Committee, and since the Committee reported several organizations, such as Mr. Gibson Jarvie's *Credit for Industry, Ltd.*, have been founded to help the enterprising small business. But it is safe to say that the problem has not yet been solved. The new organizations, quite naturally, have been unwilling to experiment at the expense of their shareholders and have found their growth correspondingly hampered.

But in the depressed areas, where all else has failed, experiment is essential. The usefulness of S.A.R.A. depends entirely on whether it can take the risk of starting out on a new line and backing the man more effectively than hitherto. Moreover it is not only necessary to " back the man," the man must first of all be found.

It is by now fairly clear that those responsible for S.A.R.A., do not regard it as their function to go out and stimulate enterprise. They are bankers ; they have set up an organization ; and now applications must come in through the recognized channels. It implies no reflection on the great tradition of British banking to say that energetic action to seek out and encourage enterprising men hardly falls within its scope.

To find the man is as vital as to back him. The only organizations at present in a position to do this are the various Development Councils.

These Councils, which consist almost entirely of leading business men, Trade Union leaders, and so on, who give their time and services for nothing, have already put in a great deal of valuable preliminary work, particularly on investigation and publicity. But neither investigation nor publicity are of much use by themselves ; they have to be thoroughly and energetically followed up. At the present time it is perhaps questionable whether the Development Councils have either the personnel or the resources for this purpose.

Let me illustrate this with a concrete case. Not long ago I happened to discover in Cleator Moor the potential basis of a toy industry such as that spontaneously suggested by the industrialist friend who visited me in

West Cumberland.   A number of men, working under the totally uncommercial guidance of a group of Roman Catholic social workers, have produced excellent wooden toys which seem to find a ready market.   But as the toys are hand-made—the necessary machinery is lacking although a Government grant has been applied for—the sales do not do more than pay expenses, and the men have now been working for nearly a year without any pay whatever.   Since they have hitherto seen little prospect of the work being put on a wage-paying basis, their keenness is falling off, and unless something is done at once the whole experiment will be abandoned.

Apparently all that has hitherto been done with regard to the toy trade is to ask the advice of a leading established toy manufacturer in the South, whose experience incidentally was not of wooden but of cheap tin toys.   Not unnaturally he gave a negative reply.

Now it seems to me that there are two possible ways of handling this problem.   One is for the Development Council to commission an energetic and able man with experience of the toy trade to make a full investigation of the possibility of developing a commercial industry on this basis.   The investigation might even include a visit to Bavaria, where a toy industry of this kind has flourished for generations.   Assuming that the investigator reached a positive conclusion, he might then be entrusted with the task of finding some enterprising person in the toy trade prepared, and with sufficient capital, to make a start.   This capital could then be supplemented with a loan from S.A.R.A.   Alternatively the investigator himself might be prepared to take on the business.

Another method would be to start by giving the experiment good publicity. Incidentally a tentative attempt on my part to do this in an article in *The Times*, which was followed up by a letter from Lord Howard of Penrith, who is personally interested in the experiment, actually produced a number of offers to endeavour to establish an industry. Once such offers have been obtained, there is surely no reason why the Development Council should not sift them out, select the most suitable man, and then see that he is fully backed by such financial assistance as is available. Some of his expenses in the experimental stage might be paid, and a more comprehensive method of training men for his purpose, of bridging the gap between the men's dependence on the dole and their receipt of full wages might be devised—there are ways of doing this even under the existing regulations.

It is, of course, quite irrelevant to my argument whether this particular experiment could be developed on a commercial basis or not. I merely put it forward as illustrating a possible method. All over the depressed areas similar experiments, many of a semi-charitable nature, have been undertaken, and some of them must certainly afford a real commercial opportunity. Unless they are put on a proper paying basis they will in the long run inevitably be abandoned.

The point to bear in mind is that for the purpose of developing new industries in the depressed areas it is often useless to approach eminent established industrialists in other districts, even for advice. Sub-consciously, at any rate, that advice is likely to be coloured by the desire common to all industrialists to prevent the development of competition. Moreover the general prejudice against the areas tends to make established men stress the difficulties of starting enterprises there.

Surely the only way out of this dilemma is to find a way of approaching the younger men in the industries concerned, men who are not yet established, who are of more elastic habit of mind than their elders, who may perhaps be dissatisfied with their position and prospects. Such men would be more likely to see opportunities and far more ready to make a move and seize them than any established industrialist. Mr. John Benn, who also made this point in some letters to *The Times* following up a recent article of mine, suggested that the younger executives of established concerns should be attracted by the guarantee of their existing earnings for a period of years. That might be difficult to arrange, but at any rate there is no reason why such men should not be commissioned to make the preliminary investigations.

To commission men for investigations and negotiations in this way would need larger resources than seem at present to be available to the Development Councils. Moreover there is another point to be considered.

If the Development Councils are to proceed on such lines they will obviously need a great deal of initiative and ability to pick men. It is one thing to put propositions before established industrialists, supporting them merely with general arguments about the suitability of the area, and another to choose rising men with initiative and help them to establish themselves. This latter method would, of course, be most effective if the Development Councils were able to suggest suitable partnerships and arrange channels of finance.

Successful action of this kind obviously calls for first-class men to carry it out, men with qualities which command very high remuneration in the open market. Considering that the Development Councils also need first-class salesmanship and that a substantial firm thinks little of paying £2,000 or £3,000 a year to its sales manager, it is perhaps open to doubt whether either the salaries or the numbers of the paid staff of the Councils are adequate for the work required.

Whether all these tasks are or are not considered to fall within the scope of the Development Councils, it must be feasible to find some way of carrying them out. Another possibility would be to form a Finance Company on lines somewhat different from those on which S.A.R.A. is run.

There can be little doubt that the plight of the depressed areas commands a public sympathy and goodwill which few other causes can command. But hitherto, apart from purely charitable appeals, there have been few attempts to capitalize this goodwill financially.

Yet the history of one such attempt shows what can be done. In his remarkable speech at the meeting inaugurating the Cumberland Development Council, Mr. St. Clare Grondona, the District Commissioner, pointed to a notable Cumbrian achievement. In 1924 a colliery in the north of Cumberland was obliged to close down. A group of people headed by a well-known local figure, Mr. Charles Roberts, took over the assets of the Company, formed a new concern, the Miners' (Industries) Trust, Ltd., and appealed for subscriptions to a capital fund, supported by a letter from Mr. Roberts in *The Times*. £30,000 was received ; the colliery and its allied enterprises were re-opened ; and more recently a start has been made on new ventures. The investors have received 5 per cent. on their money, and the value of the capital assets has increased by £33,000. Above all, some 230 men have been kept continuously in employment, and at the time of Mr. Grondona's speech they had received over £220,000 in wages.

The investors in this enterprise " for purposes of gain " may have had their 5 per cent., but they none the less rendered a public service at least as great as if they had given their money for a purely charitable purpose. They were prepared to take a chance.

It is difficult to imagine a greater service than could be rendered by a really active Finance Company for the depressed areas prepared to find the man and to back him when found. Not only might it lead, if successful, to the employment not merely of hundreds but of tens of thousands of men who would otherwise be on the dole, but in any event it could not fail to provide extraordinarily valuable lessons on the possibility of stimulating enterprise. There must be a great number of investors throughout the country with whom these considerations would have weight and who would also be prepared to take a chance for a purpose of such obvious social and national value.

Unless the whole thesis of this book is unsound it would be a good chance. If the depressed areas are really areas of opportunity, money will be made there. And there is no reason why the proposed Company should not make money ; indeed only if it does so will it be able to fulfil its purpose. It should not confine itself, like S.A.R.A., to making loans ; above all, I

believe it should take participations in the profits or
" equity " of the businesses it assists. The experience
of the great German banks, who were so largely
responsible for the development of German industry,
shows that that is the only way to compensate for the
risk of loss inherent in the foundation and nursing of
new enterprises.

A Finance Company of this kind would, of course,
need to be established under the best possible auspices,
with the backing of one or more of the leading houses
in the City. There must be nothing amateurish or
unbusinesslike about it if it is to raise enough money
to be of real use, say, at least £1,000,000. It would
have to co-operate closely with the Commissioners and
the Development Councils, but whether it should
ask assistance from the Government is a moot
point.

With the prospective compensation of a share of the
profits of successful enterprises, and with the shareholders definitely prepared to take a chance, the Company might well show itself more daring than S.A.R.A.
even without the Government guarantee against loss,
which although it amounts in the case of S.A.R.A.
to 25 per cent. of the loans made seems hardly
sufficient for its object.   But there is surely no reason
why the proposed Finance Company should not receive
the same assistance as S.A.R.A., since it would serve
the same purpose.   Competition is always a good
incentive to enterprise, and two companies serving the
needs of the Special Areas would be more effective than
one.   As Mr. Malcolm Stewart pointed out when
recommending the establishment of S.A.R.A., the saving on unemployment benefit must be set off against

the contingent loss.   There can be no doubt that the additional risk would be well worth taking.

Here are a few possible ways of stimulating enterprise.   There are many others which will occur to any intelligent business man who gives his attention to the subject.

For example, during the last few years a great many foreign industrialists have started factories in this country in order to get within the tariff barrier.   At the same time political circumstances in Germany, one of the most efficient countries in the world, have made available a wealth of industrial enterprise and talent only comparable to that of the Huguenots and the Flemish weavers in the past, and some of it has come to Great Britain.   Yet although the Government commands various means of influencing the actions of immigrant industrialists, who in any case are usually extremely anxious to secure the goodwill of the authorities in the country where they are starting business, there has been no concerted attempt to induce suitable men to come or to get those who do come to establish their businesses in the areas where they are really wanted.

Again, both Lord Portal and Sir Arthur Rose suggested in their reports that preference to the depressed areas should be given in allocating Government orders, a particularly important fact in these days of rearmament.   Here and there such preference may have been given, but the principle has certainly not been sufficiently established to make it a feature calculated to attract industrialists to the areas.

Nor has the general goodwill felt towards the depressed areas been mobilized from a marketing point of view.   The success of the " Buy British " and " Buy Empire " campaigns shows what can be done in this direction.   Why should not a definite mark of origin be authorized for goods produced within the scheduled Special Areas, and a campaign started to induce the public to " Buy SpA " ?

Ideas of this kind are the stock-in-trade of good publicity men.   To judge by results there can be little doubt that the publicity for the depressed areas has been comparatively unco-ordinated and ineffective. Publicity and " high-pressure salesmanship " are often abused for purely private ends, but they are none the less among the most powerful forces in modern economic development and experience shows that they can be equally effectively used for purposes of national importance.

If the first principle of securing recovery in the depressed areas must be to find the man and to back him, the second is to make the areas as attractive as possible to the type of man needed.

From the purely industrial point of view the development of trading, or rather manufacturing, estates on the Slough model is a step in the right direction.   When starting out on a new venture which may or may not pay, industrialists generally wish to risk as little capital as possible.   They often prefer to rent a factory, particularly one thoroughly adapted to their requirements, rather than to buy or build one.   While it may be wise to watch the results of the two estates on Tyneside and in South Wales before launching out too extensively, arrangements should be made to set up new estates, small or large, wherever there appears to be a real demand.   In particular, there is a strong case for immediate action in the other Special Areas—West Cumberland and on the Clyde.

The provision of adequate public facilities, such as water, electricity, gas, and transport is also of great importance.   While at the present time the powers of the Commissioners in co-operation with the local authorities and the existence of the grid are generally sufficient to ensure that the first three factors should not act as a deterrent to enterprise, the position as regards transport is very different.

As we have seen, the Commissioners cannot make grants for road construction since such grants are payable by the Ministry of Transport, and Mr. Malcolm Stewart clearly implied that the Ministry had been reluctant to depart from its established precedents in favour of the Special Areas.   The railways are, of course, even more difficult to move, since they are private enterprises.   Yet the road difficulty is merely a question of internal Government machinery, while the recent support the Government have granted to the railways by way of guaranteed loans ought, one would think, to have given them a certain influence.   Scarcely any of the new developments financed out of the loans were in the depressed areas.

Economic factors, however, are not the only influences on the location of industry.   We must never forget that the final decisions rest with individual business men.   If businesses are to be established in the distressed areas, managers and managing directors must be prepared to live there.

In an address to the Economics Section of the British Association at Blackpool, dealing with " the

localization of industry and the depressed areas," Mr.
S. R. Dennison, of Manchester University, expressed
doubts about this " facile generalization." Considerations of cost, he said, usually prevailed.   That may be
so.   Yet on the same day as Mr. Dennison's remarks
appeared in print the following advertisement appeared
in *The Times :*

" Wanted to purchase or rent, a modern factory of
from 100,000 sq. ft. to 200,000 sq. ft. in London suburb,
or town within 50 miles of London, having good rail
facilities and rail siding ;   must be well lighted and
drained and should be in district where skilled and
unskilled engineering labour is plentiful ;   pleasant
surroundings and social amenities for senior staff a
consideration.   Write   and   give   full   details,   with
pictures and plates if possible to Box ——."

The group of practical business men and economists
who are responsible for *Planning* disagree with Mr.
Dennison.   The issue of October 8th, 1935, points out
that " given the contemporary outlook and standard
of values, prestige accrues, on the principle that nothing
succeeds like success, to a town or region which is
flourishing and expanding, and which has money to
spend.   The prestige is enhanced if the development is
such as to make an instantly favourable impression on
the casual visitor—if there are fine buildings, bridges
and public works, spacious road approaches, and plenty
of light and life in evidence.   Always potent in drawing
the most enterprising and creative people, this factor is
becoming more potent still through the cinema, broad-
casting and the national Press.   People like to feel that
the place they are living in has a value which is recognized ;   they also like to feel in sympathy with its

atmosphere. The increase of leisure and of leisure activities makes directors and managers refuse to tie themselves to places which do not come up to their standards, and this resistance is reinforced by their wives and families, who may exercise an important indirect effect on the location of industries."

The problem is really how to place the depressed areas on the map, to get people to go there, to take an interest in them, to see their opportunities, and finally to want to live there. One way of doing this is to develop the most attractive parts of the areas as holiday and residential centres.

I do not know whether Mr. Dennison was responsible for the Manchester University Report on West Cumberland, which committed itself to the statement that the development of the district as a holiday centre would have little effect on employment. One would have thought that anything which brought money into a district, would help employment and provide opportunities, not perhaps for unemployed miners but at any rate for their sons and daughters. Moreover, once active-minded business men can be attracted to a district even on holiday, they get ideas, which may fructify when they go back to their offices. They talk to their friends. Gradually the rumour spreads that the district is a pleasant place to live in. Retired men go there and take an interest in local enterprise. Eventually an atmosphere is created in which people no longer react instinctively against any suggestion of a move to the district and, above all, a feeling of optimism is engendered both within the district and concerning it.

If there is doubt about the soundness of this argument, the way to test it is by practical experiment. And whatever the view of the Manchester University investigators may be there can be little doubt that the most suitable place to make the experiment is West Cumberland.

Here is a district with magnificent scenery and a healthy, invigorating climate. There is good and cheap fishing and shooting, some of the best seaside golfing country in England, safe bathing, and the best climbing in the country. Yet in the South this district is almost unknown. People retire or go for their holidays to the South Coast, to Scotland, to North Wales, to the lakes on the eastern side of the mountains, abroad, anywhere but to the West Cumberland coast.

This is not really surprising. For one thing the publicity for West Cumberland has been totally ineffective. This is now being remedied by the Development Council. But publicity of itself will be of little use unless a serious attempt is made to improve the facilities and amenities offered to visitors and residents.

The railway service provided by the L.M.S. is one of the worst and most uncomfortable in Great Britain. Few people who have made the night journey from Euston *via* Carnforth (where passengers are turned out of their sleepers at 5 a.m.) will want to try it again. As for motorists, their attention on the coast road from the South is so taken up by the perpetual hairpin bends that they have neither time nor energy to admire the lovely scenery. For about thirty miles along one of the finest coasts in England there is only one place that can properly be called a seaside resort, and that place rather prides itself on not possessing a cinema, nor

L

indeed any other method of whiling away a wet after-noon.

The type of enterprising business man whose interest West Cumberland needs so badly expects more than this.   He is accustomed to comfort and modern standards of hotel-keeping as well as of transport.   His wife may not climb or fish or play golf, but she dislikes being bored.   If he is attracted by publicity and subsequently disillusioned more harm than good will have been done.

The first and most obvious thing to do is to improve transport facilities.   Certain minor alterations to Carnforth Station would be of great value to Barrow as well as to West Cumberland, while another important feature would be the proposed bridge over the Duddon Estuary.   The stimulating effects of the arterial road to the North of Scotland show what a first-class coast road would be likely to do, and the lie of the ground is such that the road would spoil neither coastline nor mountains, but act as a feeder to both.   Moreover, from the point of view of light industries, the road would have an immense value as providing an easy method of lorry transport to Lancashire and the South.

The problems of amenities, hotel accommodation, and so on, could be handled by the Development Council and the Commissioner.

Financial assistance to local authorities by the Commissioner could be supplemented by loans from S.A.R.A. to suitable hotels or development syndicates —which incidentally at present S.A.R.A. seems reluctant to make.   Moreover, in one way or another, the local prejudice and lack of enterprise against which the active members of the Development Council, notably Mr. Sadler, the Chairman, and Mr. Adams, the Secretary, are waging a perpetual struggle, will have to be overcome. The Cumbrians are justly proud of the peculiar atmosphere of their county, but they cannot avert its destruction merely by ignoring world-wide trends. As *Planning* points out in the issue from which we have already quoted : " the vitality of local tradition can only be maintained by constant revaluation and self-criticism in each community. Where such self-criticism exists the stranger can become acclimatized and feel that the effort is worth while, but where there is an atmosphere of satisfaction with—or, at least, defence for—everything local and traditional because it is local and traditional, it will soon be found that people from outside cannot or will not find a foothold, while the more active-minded younger people from within the community will emigrate to a more congenial environment."

As each individual improvement comes up for consideration the argument is generally advanced that existing demands do not warrant it. The L.M.S. say that the traffic is insufficient to pay for new developments ; the Ministry of Transport take a traffic census of the present road and say that it is so little used that a new one would be wasted ; local authorities refuse to put up the simplest amenities for visitors in order to avoid raising the rates. Few people seem to consider that improvements should in the long run pay for themselves by the traffic and custom they attract.

If only piecemeal remedies are tried this obstruction-ism may have some justification. In order to produce the quick results that are so badly needed it is essential to make simultaneous and well-co-ordinated efforts along the various possible lines. This is just as true of the problem as a whole as of the question of residential and holiday amenities. Here again it is possible to make a practical experiment by devoting particular energy for a time to a limited area and watching the results. For this purpose also, West Cumberland offers a great many advantages.

Bad communications and the resultant isolation, largely a national responsibility, have made West Cumberland the Cinderella of the depressed areas. It is perhaps less likely to revive of itself than any Special Area, and it is, as we have seen, an area from which transfer is exceedingly difficult.

Yet it is a comparatively small district, readily surveyed and readily handled. It is dominated by a relatively small number of industrial concerns and great landowners, most of whom are on the Development Council. If effective influence is brought to bear in the proper quarters, the approval of everybody who matters for a comprehensive programme should be easy to obtain. And it is so rich in possibilities that, as Mr. St. Clare Grondona pointed out in the speech from which we have already quoted, " if some vast cataclysm overwhelmed every part of the world excepting only Cumberland, the native ingenuity, the imagination, the industry and the constructive skill of Cumbrians would find at their disposal virtually every material requisite to the maintenance of a high standard of living and of culture."

Above all, West Cumberland is strategically the most favourably situated industrial area in the British Isles. It is far from any possible air attack, and the difficult air currents over the hills on the east would render such an attack in the face of effective defence exceedingly precarious, while the coast offers no large rivers or other landmarks (except the Duddon estuary) for air navigation. Its harbours are on the Irish Sea, a suitable and well-protected concentration point for convoys. It has its own coal, and hematite ore, which is essential for armour plating and may well not be easy to obtain from Spain in the future. To establish an active, or at any rate a potential arms industry in such a place, seems an obvious national interest, and in the arms industry to-day Government influence is paramount.

The Commissioners and others have urgently pressed the undisputed claims of West Cumberland and South Wales from the strategic point of view on Sir Thomas Inskip and his organization. But they have had little success. The new arms factories seem to be opening in the vulnerable Midlands. Can it be that the authorities responsible for our defence policy are allowing themselves to be governed by the industrialists with whom they are co-operating ? Do they merely go to established men and accept their views and advice, their prejudices against the depressed areas ? It may be so. The experience of the War was soon forgotten. Yet if the War taught one outstanding economic lesson, it was that the direction of economic development, the concentration on nationally valuable ends, was merely a matter of taking the bull by the horns and—directing.

Another lesson of the War was the value of voluntary activities and public co-operation. It is futile to imagine that Government activity, even when directed to the end of stimulating private enterprises, will be sufficient to rehabilitate the depressed areas. Unless people within the areas are ready to pull together, and the goodwill elsewhere is properly mobilized, the efforts of the Government will largely be frittered away.

The first essential is, of course, that those with local influence and authority should refrain from unnecessary obstruction. Unfortunately there are people who pride themselves on giving their time to serve on the innumerable committees and boards through which local government is carried on in this democratic country, but none the less allow personal jealousies and prejudice and bickerings to bias their judgment and thus help to block the most obviously valuable measures.

Even more important, however, is that everybody who can do so should be ready to give positive help. There are many ways that help can be given, and I have only space to suggest a few here.

Consider, for example, the most vital problem of all, the attraction of enterprising business men to the areas. Almost everybody can help to create a pleasant social atmosphere in which the men and their wives feel themselves welcome. Then the leading personalities, landowners and others, should surely be ready to play a leading part. No one with any knowledge of the motives which sway individual men, and women, can doubt that the tactful exercise of social influence by prominent social figures—some discreet entertaining, perhaps a skilfully arranged house-party or two, for example—could do much both to get business men to visit the areas and to make them pleasant places in which to live. Unless the great families connected with the depressed areas, some of which have drawn out fabulous sums and put little back, are prepared to do something to justify their position, they cannot expect to retain it, or even in the long run to exist as a class. It is only necessary to look at the example of the Royal family, who incidentally have again and again shown their sympathy with the depressed areas and their readiness to help, to see what can be done.

It would be unfair to suggest that no goodwill has been shown by the leading and better situated classes in general. On the contrary. But that goodwill has tended to concentrate rather on charity and occasional social service than on practical measures of lasting economic value.

I do not mean to imply with this remark a reflection on the value of social service in general. We have seen from our brief study of the Totalitarian State the vast reserves of potential idealism in the world to-day and the part which organized voluntary activities can play in drawing them out. That many of those activities, like the German labour service, have by now become compulsory or semi-compulsory does not alter the fact that they were practically as valuable and effective before compulsion entered into them. Group activity is inherent in the spirit of the age ; it is an essential part of a social life in which the people as a whole are rapidly becoming the paramount factor ; and under representative or dictatorial government it is equally inescapable. The instruments by means of which most group activities are carried on in this country are the various voluntary social service bodies, and while they undoubtedly suffer from the inefficiencies and jealousies and obstructions which hamper most democratic organisms, the immense importance of their work can scarcely be overestimated.

But in their effect on the problems of employment and the depressed areas most of the existing social service activities are merely palliative. They are good palliatives ; they have, as we have seen, done much to diminish the pain of unemployment. They help to keep some spirit and efficiency in the men. They afford a magnificent opportunity for close contact and helpful co-operation between the various classes of the community ; the students and others whose Franciscan methods and practical attempts to assist unemployed men are so sympathetically recorded in Mr. John Hoyland's book, *Digging for a New England*, could hardly have had more valuable experience or have done more to create a better social atmosphere. Only in comparatively rare instances, however, does social service contribute towards the provision of regular employment, which is after all the only really satisfactory solution.

Somehow the connection between social service and productive enterprise has not yet been fully established. Business men, it is true, often take an interest in social service, but it is an interest almost entirely divorced from the practical side of their work. They give money ; they serve on committees. But business is business and charity is charity and never the twain shall meet.

Social workers, on the other hand, are too often lacking in understanding of business principles and methods. Through idealism, or perhaps through a misunderstanding of Socialist theory, some of them seem to have become imbued with a rooted distaste for " enterprises for purposes of gain." Others may be led by their sympathy for the men they are helping into much the same reserved attitude and mistrust of those in positions of authority in business and administration as is common among the unemployed men themselves. Whatever the reasons may be, social service seems rather to constitute the salvage corps of the economic system than an integral part of its machinery.

Yet really intimate co-operation between social service and the business and administrative machinery of the country could achieve a great deal. Take, for example, the experimental attempt to train men in toy-making at Cleator Moor. If those responsible for this and similar experiments could make a really whole-hearted effort to find practical business men, capable of establishing a paying enterprise, they might succeed more often than they expected. And they would have done a far greater service than by continuing on a semi-charitable basis.

Then again, social workers occupy an important strategic position between employers and prospective employees. We have seen that one of the obstacles to enterprise in the depressed areas is the largely ill-founded belief of employers in the past that the men are difficult to handle. Social workers are in a position to dispel that belief by arranging informal meetings between the working men in an area and employers who might be willing to go there, and the impression thus created could be strengthened by frank talks with the Trade Union leaders.

Much the same applies to the relations between unemployed men and the administrative officials who are dealing with them. It reflects no discredit on a body of able and hardworking men to say that social workers have opportunities of informal contact with unemployed men which are in the nature of things denied to the officials of the Labour Exchanges. They can, for example, discuss and explain the various attempts made by the Ministry of Labour to provide training for boys and men, as well as land settlement schemes and the like, and while everyone with experience of social work will know that this is difficult ground, there can be little doubt that with tactful handling of the subject a good deal can be done. At any rate to allow a sort of competition between the Ministry of Labour and voluntary schemes to develop, as sometimes happens, is obviously unsatisfactory.

Probably there is no sphere of activity in which this co-operation is more important than in the matter of labour transference. I have had many opportunities of discussing the subject with unemployed men as well as with men who have actually been transferred. All of them stressed the social aspect of transfer—the difficulty which transferred individuals and families have of making new social contacts and friendships, of fitting into the new environment.

The experience of the very active social service organization in Durham, from which county transfer has probably been more successful than from anywhere else in the depressed areas, shows the value of a connection between clubs, hostels, and community centres in the districts to which men are being transferred and social workers in the depressed areas. Nothing is more encouraging to a prospective transferee than to receive full information about such facilities together with suitable letters of introduction from a social worker, a clergyman, or anybody he knows and trusts, when he is facing a plunge into the unknown. One case within my own experience will serve as an illustration. A lad of about twenty had been transferred before, but had walked home because he "felt so lonely." I arranged with the Labour Exchange to give him another chance, furnished him with introductions, and heard recently that he is now working happily in his new environment.

Another instance of successful transfer by voluntary effort to my home village of Ewhurst, in Surrey, may also be of some interest. A special sermon was preached in the parish church, and as a result, through the Durham social service organization and the Ministry of Labour we brought down a man who had taken a short course in gardening and land work at the Hardwick Hall residential centre. By arrangement among a number of local residents we guaranteed him this type of work for a year, and with some difficulty found temporary accommodation for him and his family. Within six months he had secured permanent employment and a suitable house.

Had it not been for the housing shortage we could have done the same thing for four or five families, and in view of the shortage of local labour they would equally rapidly have been absorbed. Elsewhere in prosperous South country and Midland villages a similar condition prevails, and an experiment of the kind at Nork, also in Surrey, was the subject of a letter to *The Times* from Mr. Malcolm Stewart on March 19th, 1936. But until some Government assistance in the matter of housing is available it is obviously impossible to develop the method on the wide scale which would otherwise be possible. While it is one thing to subsidize housing in over-developed industrial districts, in order to spare industrialists the trouble of launching out where labour is available, it is quite another to organize transference in small numbers to prosperous country villages, and this might prove in the long run one of the most promising ways of settling families on the land.

This, indeed the whole question of transfer, is quite frankly a digression from our main theme of stimulating enterprise in the depressed areas. But it does perhaps help to show the almost endless possibilities of helpful co-operation that exist, both inside and outside the areas. And towards that co-operation there are few who cannot contribute something, whether they be social workers, clergymen, members of local government bodies, landowners, business men, Trade Union leaders, private citizens, and even unemployed men themselves.

What is needed in the depressed areas and in regard to their problems is something of the spirit of a crusade. Not very long ago a friend—by no means of an adventurous or militaristic temperament—told me that he had never been happier than during the War. The sense of comradeship, of co-operative purpose, the feeling that all classes were working together for a great end, had made the War worth while despite its tragedy and devastation, and now it had given place to an inglorious scramble for individual advantage. The same point was made by Mr. Delisle Burns, who argued in a remarkable article that this was one of the most important causes of war. Mr. Delisle Burns suggested a question with which I will conclude the chapter. Is the peril of war the only motive powerful enough to override egotisms and jealousies, and to call forth the united effort we need not only in the depressed areas but in tackling many other vital problems in political and economic life that are facing us to-day ?

CHAPTER VIII

CONCLUSION

WHEN I set out to write this book, those of my friends who had knowledge of the problems involved all advised me to avoid the sentimental appeal that " something should be done." I have tried to follow their advice and to make concrete suggestions, at any rate, by implication, wherever I have ventured to criticize.

The last thing I wish to claim is that these suggestions are in any sense exhaustive or even that they are all practicable ; they are no more than illustrations of the general principles put forward. That is one of the main reasons why such stress has been laid on the method of practical experiment. While it is quite impossible to indicate in advance precisely what measures will be successful, to appeal for experiment on certain definite lines is surely something rather different from the vague sentimentalism against which my friends' warning was directed.

Above all, however, I have endeavoured to make three fundamental points as a basis for action and experiment. The first point is that the problem of employment lies at the very root of all our economic troubles, and consequently that it calls for a greater concentration of attention and effort than any other.

The second point is that it should be tackled at its "hard core," and primarily in the depressed areas. The third point is that the stimulation and direction of "enterprises for purposes of gain" is the only practical way to achieve satisfactory results.

The supreme importance of employment can scarcely be questioned. We traced some of its fluctuations in the past ; we saw that the lack of it, unemployment, was an outstanding feature of the great transitional periods of crisis which have punctuated the economic progress of mankind ; we found that the capitalist system had made less progress towards solving the problem than in any direction ; we noted that unemployment was probably never so severe nor so widely spread as it is to-day ; and we learnt from some of the Totalitarian States what catastrophic effects can result from the failure to provide work.

Nor will there, I hope, be much disagreement with the view that the depressed areas are the places to tackle in the first instance. Certainly no one who tried our motor-run from West Cumberland to Durham would venture to dispute this. All that can be said is that the depressed areas, or rather the scheduled Special Areas, only contain about 300,000 unemployed as compared with a total of over 1,600,000 on the register.

We have, however, seen a good many reasons for supposing that the recovery of the depressed areas would have an effect on the general problem of unemployment quite out of proportion to the relative numbers involved. Here is concentrated a large proportion of the intractable "hard core," notably the unhappy victims of "structural unemployment."

Indeed, if we include for the purposes of the argument all the important non-scheduled areas where there is serious unemployment, it is probable that the great majority of the really deserving " hard core " cases could be covered ; the remaining cases in other areas would consist very largely of men who either through misfortune, advancing age, or through their own fault, could not readily be fitted into productive employment.

Even more important is the fact that the depressed areas are economically speaking the least " saturated " of all districts in Great Britain.   They have far more potentialities, more unexploited opportunities, than the prosperous districts.   Not only is development in the prosperous districts being, as we noted, increasingly hampered by the shortage of labour and the high price of land, but the very fact that they are prosperous has attracted many business men to them who must have seized at any rate the most obvious opportunities.

Hitherto, on the other hand, the depressed areas have attracted nobody ; neither their productive nor their marketing possibilities have been properly exploited, nor for that matter properly explored.   Ample labour is available : land and buildings are cheap.   The present purchasing power of the population is extremely low, and as the dole gives place to wages will rapidly increase.   The Northern areas are close to the great centres of population where activity is already being stimulated by rearmament and where progress is now much more rapid than in the South, so that expanding markets should be available near the areas as well as within them.   If these arguments, which led us to call the depressed areas the areas of opportunity, are sound, it seems obvious that once a real start is made the self-acting and cumulative effects of economic development should show themselves far more speedily than would be the case elsewhere.

A great increase of demand from within the depressed areas would, of course, have a considerable effect on prosperity in other districts. The areas could not possibly satisfy their demands themselves. Moreover the saving on the dole would translate itself into increased purchasing power elsewhere, either through reduced taxation or through other Government expenditure. The argument which is sometimes advanced to the effect that to encourage new industries in the depressed areas means putting men out of employment elsewhere is based on wholly false economic premises.

Certainly industrialists may sometimes be affected by competition from the depressed areas ; indeed, we hoped they would be in order to make them pay attention to the advantages of the areas. But, at any rate, as long as the present up-swing of the trade cycle continues, any labour put out of work in the prosperous districts is likely to be rapidly re-absorbed. The labour shortage is at present preventing the establishment and development of still newer industries there, so that there can be little fear that the slack will not be taken up.

Will the up-swing continue, however ?   In a recent lecture to the British Association Sir William Beveridge, speaking with all the authority of the chairman of the Statutory Committee on Unemployment Insurance, committed himself to the statement that cyclical unemployment was practically non-existent. The 1,600,000 unemployed consisted of the " hard core," of sufferers from " structural " unemployment, and

M

a million or so " seasonal " or " interval " unemployed, which seems to represent a practically
irreducible minimum of 8 per cent. as opposed to the
2 per cent. of Trade Union unemployment generally
regarded as irreducible before the War.   While Sir
William could not state with certainty whether this
was a real increase of unemployment or only the result
of a more complete record, he was convinced that " it
would not be prudent to allow for an increase in unemployment of less than 6 per cent.—say 800,000—or to
assume that it can be many years distant."

If Sir William is right we are faced with the prospect
of seeing the next cyclical depression carry unemployment practically up to the worst figure reached during
the recent slump, without there being much chance of
improvement in the meantime.   Indeed, the only
prospect of improvement he held out was an attack
on the "hard core" mainly through the depressed
areas.

But unless we accept the fatalistic view that the
movements of the trade cycle are fixed and unalterable,
we can find good grounds for believing that the revival
of the depressed areas would have an important effect
on the present recovery movement.   Let us go back
for a moment to our theoretical discussion in Chapter
III.   We saw that crises and the subsequent depressions
occur when business men have been competing among
themselves to borrow and invest and have thus forced
up interest rates and prices.   To-day, however, plenty
of idle capital is still awaiting investment so that
interest rates remain low and the credit situation shows
no signs of strain.   The rise in the general level of
wholesale prices is as yet no more than a return to

normality after the slump. The chief danger seems to be that Dr. Hayek's game of pull devil pull baker will develop as a result of the competing demands of rearmament and recovery on an industrial mechanism handicapped by the shortage of labour and the high price of land, buildings, etc., in the districts where industries have elected to establish themselves.

If, however, we can extend activity to the depressed areas we can greatly enlarge the field over which these competing demands are being exercised. We can postpone the rapid rise of prices which may otherwise set in, and incidentally keep down the cost of rearmament. In fact we can lengthen the duration of the business up-swing and broaden its base.

In that case, quite apart from the direct effect on the " hard core," the " irreducible minimum " might also find itself reduced. For if only the general improvement goes on long enough, employers will gradually be forced to take on, for example, the older men (their unwillingness to do so was stressed by Sir William) and others whom they do not now consider suitable. There will be time for training and transference schemes to take effect. And it is not impossible that we may make progress in the meantime towards controlling to some extent the trade cycle itself.

Turning again to Chapter III, we may remember that Mr. Keynes was the most optimistic of our theorists and one whom Mr. John Strachey carefully refrained from dissecting. We saw that the central feature of his theory and the one most widely accepted is that the trade cycle depends on fluctuations of the volume of investment. His main remedy is to balance the periodical shrinkages in private investment by public investment through "loan-expenditure," and we noted that the remedy was less generally approved than the diagnosis.

But what if we can effectively influence private investment ?   That is, after all, the essence of the proposals for the depressed areas which we have been discussing.   They do not embody public works merely for the sake of providing work, whose ill-effects wherever they have been tried during the last century or so we noted. Nor do they envisage such works merely as a method of spending borrowed money.   The proposals consider public works and expenditure in the same light as almost everything else—as means to the end of stimulating " enterprises for purposes of gain."

Here we come to my third point, which is likely to be far more widely disputed than either of the first two. Yet I am only trying to face the facts.   Enterprises for purposes of gain, inspired by the energy and initiation of individuals, are, and for the present are likely to remain, the basis of the economic system.

It is, of course, possible to say with Mr. John Strachey and many others that nothing can be done as long as this situation continues.   The whole-hog Marxian diagnosis may be right.   But we saw that Soviet Russia does not as yet provide conclusive evidence of its truth, and in the same chapter we gained some idea of the dangers of a direct attempt to put Marxian theory into practice.

Whatever our views may be about the ideal structure of economic life, surely in a democratic State which values its free institutions, its method of working by unfettered argument and public discussion, it is wisest to take the structure as it stands and to endeavour to mould it to our ends rather than to risk the bitter and possibly bloody struggles any attempt at a violent overturn would be likely to call forth ?

But we must be prepared to experiment in the exercise of social control, or at any rate of social influence, over economic development. Business men, owners of property, who kick against the pricks of what is to-day a universal trend, cannot expect to retain their positions in the face of the growing influence and consciousness of the broad masses of the people.

I do not believe that more than a very small section of people in any class really feel themselves wedded to a theoretical economic or social system. But there is an instinctive and almost universal feeling that things are not right as they are, that we are failing for lack of understanding and firmness of purpose to make use of the vast opportunities within our reach. In the long run that feeling will inevitably have its effect.

That the depressed areas present us with an unparalleled opportunity for showing firmness of purpose and gaining understanding is surely evident. They are, as it were, a microcosm of the nation. If we can solve their problems, whether of productive enterprise or of free and representative government, we shall be in a far better position to solve those problems for the nation as a whole.

We have seen that in spite of Commissioners, propaganda, and speeches in Parliament, the position in the depressed areas is little better than before public attention was focussed upon it. And one of the most serious dangers is that now, with reviving prosperity elsewhere, public attention is waning ; it is being directed towards other issues, notably the international situation.

Yet are not the two issues very closely related ? Not very long ago I was discussing with a group of working men, mostly unemployed, the problems of war and peace. One of them summed up the whole discussion when he said, rather wistfully, that he only wished he knew something worth dying for. Until the " man in the street," for example in the Frizington Street, feels that a whole-hearted attempt to deal with his social and economic difficulties, and above all with the problem of unemployment, is being made, is he likely to obey the statesman who, from the relative security of Whitehall, tells him to defend his " King and Country," or even the League of Nations. Or will he be suspicious lest under those high-sounding words should be concealed the interests of the industrialists and business men who would not or could not provide a proper means of livelihood ?

Faced by the Totalitarian States, which can count on the whole-hearted allegiance of their people, democracies can only hold their own if they are equally sure of their ground at home. And, above all, I believe that success in putting our own economic and social house in order by open discussion and peaceful agreement would be the most effective lead we can give towards the goal so well described by Mr. H. A. L. Fisher in the third volume of his *History of Europe* : " Europe, then, has now reached a point at which it would seem, as never so clearly in past history, that two alternative and sharply contrasted destinies await her. She may travel down the road to a new war or, overcoming passion, prejudice, and hysteria, work for a permanent organization of peace. In either case the human spirit is armed with material power. The developing miracle of science is at our disposal to use or abuse, to make or to mar. With science we may lay civilization in ruins or enter into a period of plenty and well-being the like of which has never been experienced by mankind."